EARLY HISTORY OF CEYLON

THE EARLY HISTORY OF CEYLON

AND ITS RELATIONS WITH INDIA AND OTHER FOREIGN COUNTRIES

G. C. MENDIS

WITH A FOREWORD BY
PROF. WILHELM GEIGER

THREE MAPS AND SIXTEEN ILLUSTRATIONS

GYAN

Published by

Gyan Publishing House
5, Ansari Road
Daryaganj, New Delhi-110002
Phone: 011-47034999, 9811692060
E-mail: books@gyanbooks.com

Distribution Network
gyanbooks.com
India, USA, Canada, UK, Australia, France

ISBN : 978-81-212-3339-2 (PB)
First Published, 1932

2nd Impression 2020

Printed at: Gyan Press, Delhi.

Early History of Ceylon
Author: G. C. Mendis

PREFACE

I HAVE attempted in this book to satisfy, as far as possible, the need for a work on the early history of Ceylon. I have made it my aim to eliminate all myths and legends, and base my history only on facts which are fairly certain. I cannot say that I have been altogether successful. To the research student many of the statements about the early history of Ceylon appear as problems to be investigated, rather than as facts on which a stable structure can be erected.

This book, therefore, does not pretend by any means to be exhaustive or correct in all its details. It will take a long time before it will be possible to write such a history, as the amount of research yet to be done is very great. Though the *Mahāvaṁsa* has been edited and translated with critical notes, most of the other literary works have not received sufficient attention at the hands of scholars. A large number of inscriptions have still to be edited and published, and therefore even this certain source of information cannot yet be fully exploited. The archæological work, too, has not advanced very far, and has never been carried out with such thoroughness as in India. Even a greater part of Anurādhapura has yet to be excavated, and there are a number of other places, which, when explored and excavated, are bound to yield useful results.

I am indebted to the work of many for my information, but it is not possible to mention all of them here. I cannot, however, omit to acknowledge the use I have made of *A Short History of Ceylon* by Mr. H. W. Codrington, and the English translation of the *Cūlavaṁsa*, with critical notes, by Professer Wilhelm Geiger. I have to thank Prof. R. Marrs,

Prof. S. A. Pakeman, the Rev. E. C. Dewick, the Rev. Dr. Isaac Tambyah, the Rev. F. Kingsbury, Mr. L. E. Blazé, Mr. J. L. C. Rodrigo, Mr. L. J. Gratiaen, Mr. A. M. K. Cumaraswamy, Bhikkhu Nārada, Mr. E. H. van der Wall, and the Rev. C. H. S. Ward for their criticisms and suggestions. My thanks are also due to Mr. S. Paranavitana, for the invaluable help he gave me in various ways; and to Professor Geiger, for writing the Foreword.

The picture of the Väddas is taken from Seligmann's *Veddas*, with the kind permission of the Cambridge University Press. All the other illustrations were obtained from the Archæological Department. The maps were drawn by Mr. D. J. Lokugē.

For the spelling of names of persons and places I have followed a uniform system, though sometimes it differs from the way in which the words are popularly spelt. In the case of names of kings and places I have adopted the forms most popular among the people, without keeping strictly either to the Pāli or the Siṅhalese forms of these names; but all of them are given in Appendix I.

G. C. MENDIS.

Marian Cottage,
Dehiwala, Ceylon.
August, 1932.

FOREWORD

By Prof. W. Geiger, of Munich

It is a well-known fact that for hardly any part of the continent of India is there such an uninterrupted historical tradition as for the island of Ceylon. This tradition up to the year A.D. 362 is contained in the two Pāli chronicles, the *Dīpavaṁsa* and the *Mahāvaṁsa*, but the *Mahāvaṁsa* was continued later on up to the eighteenth century, by diverse authors at diverse times, so that now it comprises the whole history of the island, from the first immigration of the Āryans under Vijaya till the arrival of the English. This chronicle is supplemented, and sometimes also corrected, by a large number of works composed in the Pāli or the Siṁhalese language. But it would be a great mistake to assume that a simple extract from these books would yield true history, for they all require a constant and penetrative criticism. Their authors are often one-sided, and lay stress on things which are of less importance to the historian than other events which they have passed over in silence. This does by no means involve upon them the reproach of lack of sincerity; for it is quite intelligible for instance, that a *bhikkhu*—and the compilers of the various parts of the *Mahāvaṁsa* were all *bhikkhus*—has deeper interest in the rise and the decline of his Church than in secular affairs. Moreover, the tradition of the oldest period is wrapped up in myths and legends, and it is very difficult to find out their historical kernel. In judging the more recent parts of the Chronicle, we ought not to forget that the whole *Mahāvaṁsa* is a *kāvya*, subject to all the rules of *alaṅkāra* valid in Indian literature; and that always more ancient *kāvyas* served as models for later compositions. Finally, regarding the historical books outside the *Mahāvaṁsa*, we should always keep in mind whether the divergent or the supplementary information contained therein is taken from a trustworthy source or is simply inventions and fictions of their respective compilers.

Under such circumstances, it is a real pleasure for me to write this Foreword to the work of Dr. G. C. Mendis. For when I read the manuscript, I saw with great satisfaction that this History of Ceylon is written by a scholar who looks at the historical tradition with critical eyes. Eliminating all legends and doubtful information, he has based his description on facts which are certain or at least probable. Moreover, he has not confined himself to a mere enumeration of events and names and chronological dates, but has also tried to describe the whole mental and economic culture, agriculture and commerce, art and literature, of the Siṁhalese, and their development from their beginnings up to the modern period. Thus Dr. Mendis' book will be a rich source of interesting information to all its readers; and this information is reliable, as far as this is possible under the present conditions. I myself, though I may sometimes dissent from the author in minor details, have read the manuscript with great pleasure and advantage, and I trust the book will find as many friends and admirers as it deserves.

München-Neubiberg,
August, 1932.

WILH. GEIGER.

CONTENTS

ILLUSTRATIONS

MAPS

CHAPTER I

THE HISTORY OF ANCIENT AND MEDIEVAL CEYLON

1. *The Mahāvaṅsa.* The chief source used for the writing of this history of ancient and medieval Ceylon is the *Mahāvaṅsa*, an epic written in the Pāli language. Its first part, which relates the history of Ceylon from its legendary beginnings to the end of the reign of Mahasen (A.D. 362), was composed at the Mahāvihāra, in Anurādhapura, by a Buddhist *bhikkhu*, or monk, about the sixth century A.D. The age of its oldest available manuscript, written on *ola* leaves, is perhaps not more than two hundred years, but its text was more or less fixed by a *ṭīkā*, or commentary, written about the twelfth century A.D. The second part of the *Mahāvaṅsa*, or the *Cūlavaṅsa*, as it is sometimes called, consists of three parts. The first of these three parts (Chs. XXXVII, 51–LXXIX, 84), which continues the story to the end of the reign of Parākramabāhu I (A.D. 1186), was composed early in the thirteenth century, most probably at Polonnaruva, by a Buddhist *bhikkhu* called Dharmakīrti. The date and the author of the second part (Chs. LXXIX, 85–XC, 102), which ends with Parākramabāhu IV, are not known, but it must have been written later than A.D. 1333, as the narrative is continued up to this year. The third part was composed in the reign of Kīrti Śrī Rājasiṅha (A.D. 1747–1781), probably by the Buddhist *bhikkhu*, Tibbotuvāvē Sumaṅgala, who continued the epic up to this time.[1]

[1] Geiger, *The Indian Historical Quarterly*, Vol. VI, p. 205, and *Zeitschrift für Indologie und Iranistik Band*, VII, p. 259.

The *Mahāvaṅsa* thus gives the history of Ceylon from its beginnings up to the middle of the eighteenth century, or to the conquest of Ceylon by the British, if the supplement added in 1877 is included. Few countries possess such an unbroken record, and no part of India has such a valuable source for the reconstruction of its history. Nevertheless, what the *Mahāvaṅsa* records is mainly traditional history, and its statements have to be carefully examined before they are accepted as historical evidence.

2. *Vijaya to Duṭugämunu.* According to one account of the Dīpavaṅsa (an older Pāli chronicle in verse compiled about the fourth century A.D.), the Mahāvihāra, the records of which formed the basis of the *Mahāvaṅsa*, was built by Saddhā Tissa, the brother of Duṭugämunu, and according to both chronicles the *Aṭṭhakathā*, or the commentaries, of which the historical tradition formed a part, were put into writing in the reign of Saddhā Tissa's son, Vaḷagambā (Vaṭṭa Gāmaṇi Abhaya), who lived in the latter part of the first century B.C. An examination of the *Mahāvaṅsa* shows that its information is generally reliable only from the reign of Saddhā Tissa, and it is most likely, as the chronicles say, that definite records began to be kept only from the time of Vaḷagambā.

The events recorded about kings prior to Saddhā Tissa are wrapped in myth and legend, and it is no easy task to unravel the stories and lay bare the truth that underlies them. Perhaps on this account too much has been made of these stories, and far too many incidents related have been regarded as events that actually took place. In recent times there has been a tendency on the part of some to reject most of the events related about Vijaya and Paṇḍukābhaya as mythical, and accept as correct the *Mahāvaṅsa* story in the main from the time of Dēvānaṅpiya Tissa. There is no doubt that the *Mahāvaṅsa* has more of history in it from the time of Dēvānaṅpiya Tissa, but there is no ground for accepting the story as correct from the time of this monarch leaving out only those passages which are obviously fictitious. No independent record of any description outside Ceylon, for instance, supports the view held in Ceylon that Mahinda was a son of Aśōka. On the other hand, researches carried out in recent times into the legends of Aśōka tend to confirm the judgment of Oldenberg, who some decades ago looked upon the story of Mahinda's parentage as a pure invention.[1] The building of the Ruvanväli Säya and the Lōhapāsāda (the Brazen Palace) is attributed in the *Mahāvaṅsa* to Duṭugämunu, but the accounts in the *Dīpavaṅsa* and the *Mahāvaṅsa* themselves, when critically examined, give sufficient room to doubt this statement. The *Dīpavaṅsa* and the *Mahāvaṅsa* also do not agree with regard to the persons who erected some of the other pre-Christian buildings. Nor is there a complete list in the *Mahāvaṅsa* of the buildings put up during this time. The Kälaniya Dāgäba was one of the most famous of the ancient *dāgäbas*, but the *Mahāvaṅsa* does not say when or by whom it was built.

3. *Saddhā Tissa to Mahasen.* From the first century onwards we are on safer ground. The dynastic lists of rulers from Saddhā Tissa (77–59 B.C.) to Mahasen (A.D. 334–362) are generally confirmed by inscriptions, and they probably formed a part of the most ancient records.

The accounts of buildings erected from this time also seem to be more accurate, as there is generally no disagreement as before between the *Dīpavaṅsa* and the *Mahāvaṅsa* with regard to the persons who built them. It is likely that the dynastic lists, with the length of the reign of each king, were first kept and that the legends about persons and the traditional accounts of buildings were added later.

4. *Kit Siri Mevan to Parākramabāhu I.* A good deal of the

[1] Pryzuluski, *La Legende de L'Empéreur Aśōka.*

information of the first part of the *Cūlavaṅsa* also deals with pious acts, such as the erection of religious buildings and legends and stories of doubtful historical value related mainly for purposes of edification. But the account in the main seems to be correct, as it is often confirmed by inscriptions, both Ceylon and Indian, as well as by foreign literature.

The reign of Parākramabāhu I, the hero of the writer of this part, is described at length. Parākramabāhu is made to appear a sort of ideal king, and is credited even with miraculous performances. His virtues are sometimes exaggerated and facts unfavourable to him are occasionally suppressed. Moreover, as the *Cūlavaṅsa* was meant to be an epic or a *kāvya*, the author has not hesitated to add from his own knowledge of Sanskrit literature such matter as would adorn the poem. Nevertheless, it is clear that the account is only an adaptation of the actual events that took place, as the statements are generally supported by Ceylon and Indian inscriptions, literary works, and ancient monuments.[1]

5. *Vijayabāhu II to Parākramabāhu VIII.* The second part of the *Cūlavaṅsa* is similar to the first part in most respects. The third part is short, and gives little or no information as to certain kings. The account of the reign of Parākramabāhu II, the hero of the writer of the second part, occupies a good deal of space, but as a historical record it is even less satisfactory than that of the reign of Parākramabāhu I.

6. *The Chronology.* The dates in the *Mahāvaṅsa* are reckoned from the traditional date of the death of the Buddha, which, according to calculations made from dates given in Indian and Greek records and the *Mahāvaṅsa*, is considered to have taken place in 483 B.C. According to reckonings made in medieval times in Ceylon, the date of the

[1] Geiger, *Cūlavaṃsa*, Eng. Trs., p. vi.

death of the Buddha falls in 543 B.C. This gives a difference of about sixty years, which must have been due to an alteration made by someone, if it did not occur owing to wrong reckonings of fractions of years. Professor Geiger thinks the mistake was due to an adjustment made in the dates at the beginning of the first part of the *Cūlavaṅsa*, and he corrects the error by deducting these sixty years from the reigns of Kit Siri Mevan (Kīrti Srī Meghavarṇa), Deṭu Tis II (Jeṭṭha Tissa), and Buddhadāsa.

The round numbers, in which most of the reigns at the beginning are given, reveal their fictitious nature; and probably the dates, too, have some reality only from the reign of Saddhā Tissa or his brother, Duṭugämunu. The dates of even kings from Saddhā Tissa up to Vijayabāhu I can be taken only as approximate. The chronology of the second and third parts of the *Cūlavaṅsa* is also far from definite. The number of years some of the kings ruled is not given, and the reckonings are further complicated by the fact that more than one king ruled at the same time.

7. *Other Sources.* The *Mahāvaṅsa*, since it is primarily a religious work, is far from adequate to reconstruct the political and economic history of this island. Therefore the information gathered from it has been supplemented from other sources. For the period from Vijaya to Duṭugämunu information has been sought from the writings of geologists, zoologists, anthropologists, and ethnographists; but the results obtained were small, as apart from the studies of the Väddas, the work of these in Ceylon is still at a very elementary stage.

For the later periods much more information has been found. The Pāli and the Siṅhalese literary works, such as the *Mahābodhivaṅsa*, the *Pūjāvaliya* and the *Nikāya Saṅgraha* not only confirm, but also add to the information in the *Mahāvaṅsa*. There are also accounts left by foreign writers like the Chinese pilgrim, Fa-Hsien, and the Arab traveller, Ibn Batuta, which have helped to some extent to fill in gaps left by other works. Inscriptions, both Ceylon and Indian, give a good deal of information about kings, wars, and the maintenance of Buddhist *vihāras* (monasteries). The coins have been specially helpful in tracing Ceylon's connections with foreign countries. The ancient monuments and works dealing with them have helped considerably to note foreign influences and developments in life and thought in Ceylon.

8. *Conceptions of History.* The main defects of the *Mahāvaṁsa* as a history, as one would expect, are due to the fact that it was composed by people whose ideas of what a history should be was quite different from ours. The *Mahāvaṁsa* falls more or less within the category of histories of the earliest stage, which consisted of epic poems, legends of heroes and of wise and good men, of genealogies and dynastic lists.

The histories even of the next stage did not come up to our standards. They were written mainly in order to teach practical lessons. *The History of the Peloponnesian War* by the Greek writer, Thuycidides, and *The Temporal and Spiritual Conquest of Ceylon* by the Portuguese writer, Queyroz, belong to this class. These works not only provide a good deal of material for the reconstruction of history, but also attempt to explain the underlying causes of events. They are, however, defective, because the selection of material and the interpretation of events depended much on the personal views and the aims of the writers. They also often reveal a tendency to uphold a particular view of life or to support the views of a definite political party.

Today the main object of an historian is to interpret human development. He not only accepts the view of the unity of the human race, but also notices a definite connection between the present and the past. He sees that the present is the result of an infinite series of past events, and he explains how man gradually developed to be what he is to-day. He is not satisfied with a knowledge of kings, their successions, their wars, and their dealings with their subjects, but is interested also in the political development of peoples as well as in changes in their ideas and in their social and economic life.

9. *The Periods of History.* To explain this development, it is customary to divide history into different periods. True, there are no such strict divisions in actual history. But at the same time man's ideas and his conditions of life go through a process of change, when new forces begin to exercise their influence upon him. Then the existing system of life breaks up to a greater or lesser extent, giving place to a new order of things. This system in turn lasts till fresh ideas and other conditions lead to further changes. The time in which any set of conditions is dominant is roughly taken as a period of history, as such divisions help to give a clearer idea of the stages of development through which man has passed.

10. *The Periods of the History of Ceylon.* The history of man is sometimes divided into different stages, such as the hunting stage, the pastoral stage, the agricultural stage, the commercial stage, and the industrial stage. The history of Ceylon, too, can be divided into most of these stages. The few Väddas still left show that when they first came to Ceylon they were in the hunting stage. The Āryan settlers introduced into Ceylon the agricultural stage of development, and the Portuguese and the Dutch the commercial stage; and since the coming of the British, Ceylon has begun to enter upon the industrial stage of development.

Such divisions, however, do not give a sufficient idea of the stages of development through which Ceylon has passed. The first stage of the history of Ceylon, of which we have any definite evidence, was when the Väddas, a people who lived by hunting, were the sole inhabitants of the island. The next stage began with the coming of the Āryans, who introduced agriculture and gradually absorbed a part of the Vädda population and the Dravidians who had come to Ceylon. The third stage opened with the introduction of Buddhism, which brought Ceylon into direct contact with the Aśōkan civilisation. Then the people of Ceylon put up buildings of brick, began to carve in stone, learnt the art of writing, and benefited by the teachings of Buddhism. About the fourth century A.D. Ceylon went through a further great change. New forms of sculpture came into existence. Larger tanks were built. Pāli was more widely studied, and there was a good deal of literary activity. These changes were probably due to the influence of the social and cultural movements which took place in India under the Gupta kings in the fourth century A.D., and also to Ceylon's contact with other countries, from Italy in the west to China in the east. Then the development of the people was checked by the invasions of the Chōḷians from South India and their occupation of a part of this island, but the Siṅhalese revived again under the Polonnaruva kings, and made further progress in architecture, sculpture, literature and agriculture. Then the invasions of the Pāṇḍyans from South India, the Portuguese, the Dutch, and finally the British, gradually led to the loss of the independence of the Siṅhalese people. South Indian invaders, Chōḷians and Pāṇḍyans, have left their mark on our architecture and sculpture. The Portuguese have left behind the Roman Catholic Church, and the Dutch their system of law. The British administrative system, helped by the great changes brought about by the modern industrial civilisation, helped Ceylon to be unified and the people to progress once more. Today the Ceylonese people are on their way to take back the destinies of their country into their own hands under a democratic form of government.

11. *The Bearing of Geography on History.* The activities of these various peoples were controlled to a certain extent by the geographical conditions of the country, which in ancient and medieval times influenced to a great extent even their character and their occupations. Therefore, to understand correctly the history of Ceylon we have to keep in mind its important geographical facts, such as its physical features, the fertility of its soil, its proximity to India, its insular position, and its situation on the highway of sea traffic from the west to the east.

The fertility of the soil attracted from the earliest times peaceful immigrants and ruthless invaders, while the open plains reaching far into the interior, and the absence of any mountain ranges along the coast, made access and occupation easy. The mountainous district in the centre helped to a great degree to preserve the Siṅhalese civilisation and to save for a time many a lost cause, though it made political unity difficult in times when there were not the modern means of communication. The heavy rainfall, the dense forests, the arrangement of the river-system, and the paucity of land suitable for rice-cultivation in the south-western part of Ceylon, show why this region was the last to be occupied, while the position of the Mahaväli Gaṅga reveals why the kings of Anurādhapura exercised their power earlier over the eastern and the south-eastern parts of Ceylon.

12. *Ceylon and India.* Ceylon's proximity to India explains why its history is so much bound up with the social, economic, and cultural developments in that sub-continent. The main religions of the people, Buddhism and Hinduism, came from India. The Siṅhalese and the Tamil scripts and the Siṅhalese and the Tamil languages are derived from the same source. Siṅhalese literature, in subject-matter and style, shows itself strongly influenced by Pāli and Sanskrit literature. The Ceylon styles of architecture and sculpture can also in

the main be traced to India. Even in recent times, most of the administrative and political reforms have followed similar changes there.

At the same time Ceylon's insular position and its place in the Indian Ocean, on the route to Australia and the Far East, has helped Ceylon to develop to some extent a distinct civilisation. Buddhism, which has had a strong influence in civilising the people, might not have survived the encroachments of Hinduism had Ceylon formed a part of the mainland of India. The Portuguese and the Dutch might not have cared to conquer the maritime provinces of Ceylon but for its central position between Arabia and China; and had Ceylon not been separated from India by Palk Strait the Portuguese might not have succeeded in establishing so firmly the Roman Catholic Church and the Dutch their legal system, and drawn this island away to some extent from the currents of Indian movements.

CHAPTER II

THE BEGINNINGS

I. The Early Settlers

13. *The Pre-historic Age.* The earliest records of the activities of man are ancient implements which have lasted up to the present day. The oldest of these are fragments of rock chipped off with other stones, used by early man in his struggle against nature and wild animals. The age in which these stone implements were used is called the Stone Age, and this Stone Age is further divided into the palæolithic or the Old Stone Age, and the neolithic or the New Stone Age.

The earliest implements so far discovered in Ceylon are those of quartz, of chert, and of shell, and belong to the palæolithic age. These were no doubt once used by human beings, as they have been discovered in places to which they could have been removed only by man. We are not sure who used these stone implements, but there is reason to think that the Väddas used them before they learnt the use of iron from the Āryan settlers.

14. *The Väddas.* The Väddas, or hunters, are a short, wavy-haired, long-headed race, with moderately long faces and moderately broad noses. They belong to the same racial stock as the pre-Dravidian jungle tribes of South India, such as the Irulas and the Kurumbas. They are said also to be racially connected with the Toalas of the Celebes and the Batin of Sumatra.

According to available evidence, they were the first race of people that came to Ceylon. Their original home has not yet been discovered, and it is also not known when and how they came here, or how their kinsmen spread as far as Australia. It is probable that, like the wild animals that came from South India to Ceylon, the Väddas occupied this island at a time when these regions were not separated from each other, as now, by a stretch of sea.

At the time the Väddas came here they were, as a few of them still are, in the hunting stage of man's development. They lived in caves in the rainy season and near the river beds in the dry season. They hunted wild animals with bows and arrows, and used their flesh for food. For clothes they used garments of *riṭi* bark or of leaves. They led their life in clans, and the unit of the clan was not the individual but the family. Their religion took the form of propitiation of the spirits of the dead, and was a kind of ancestor worship.

The Väddas by no means had an easy existence. They were often not sure of their food and were constantly in danger of their life. They had to shift from place to place, according to the movements of the wild animals, and their time was taken up so much in providing themselves with the bare means of existence that they found hardly any leisure for other pursuits of life.

Therefore they were able to make hardly any contribution to the civilisation of Ceylon. Their chief service lay in the help they rendered in forming the Siṅhalese race. The Āryans when they first came to Ceylon must have married Vädda women, as they could not have brought a sufficient number of women of their own. According to Dr. Seligmann, who has made the most thorough study of the Väddas, the up-country Siṅhalese have absorbed a considerable amount of Vädda blood. This mixture probably took place as the Väddas adopted agriculture, learned the Siṅhalese language, and came into touch with the Siṅhalese community. Dr. Seligmann is also of opinion that the Bandāra cult among the Kandyans, which consists of making offerings to deceased

SHELL, CHERT, AND QUARTZ

(*Page 11*)

A ROCK SHELTER OF THE VEDDAS

(*Page 12*)

THE DEVELOPMENT OF THE SIṄHALESE SCRIPT

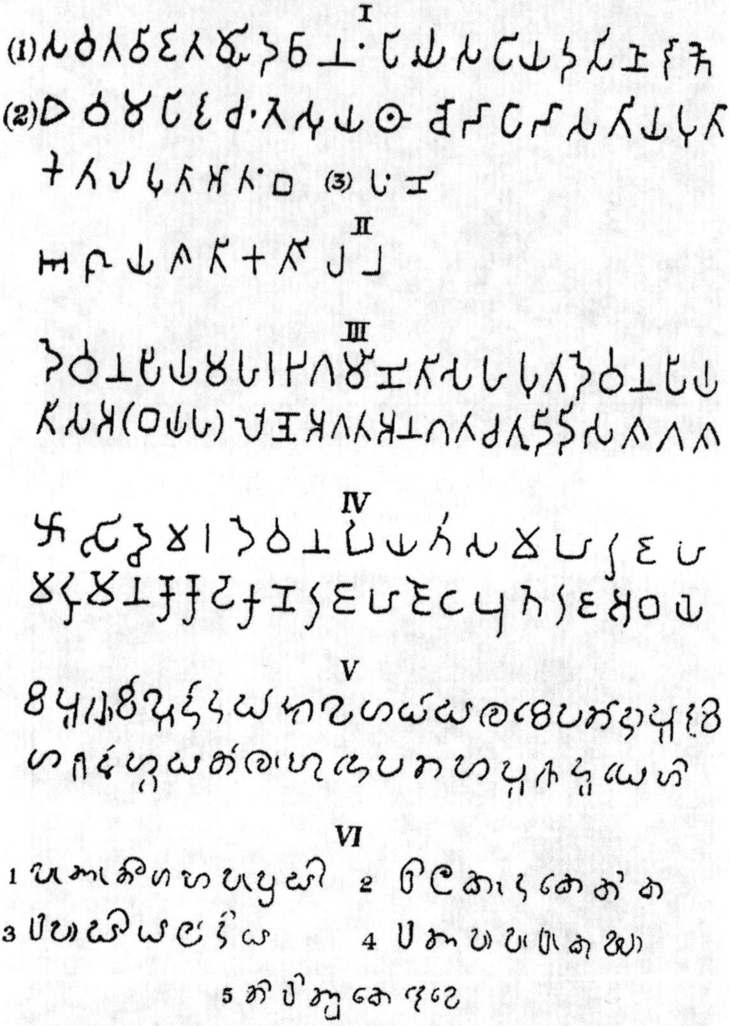

(*Page 21*)

(*See Appendix II, p. 89*)

chiefs and prominent ancestors, is a remnant of the Vädda practice of propitiating the dead.

15. *The Original Home of the Āryans.* Next to the Väddas, the people of whose settlement in Ceylon we have some definite evidence are the Āryans. The original place from which they spread into different parts of Asia and Europe has not yet been definitely located. As far back as 1767, a Frenchman showed the connection between Sanskrit and some European languages. Later Sir William Jones pointed out that Sanskrit, Persian, Greek, Latin, Celtic, and Gothic belonged to the same family of languages. Since then there has been much speculation with regard to the original home of the people who spoke Indo-European, the parent of all these languages. Some have located it in Central Asia, some in South Russia, some in North Germany, and others in Hungary.

16. *The Āryans in India and Ceylon.* The Āryans, from whatever region they started their wanderings, entered India long before 1000 B.C. The *Ṛigveda*, a collection of their earliest poems, gives us some idea of their life and customs when they were living in the Indus valley. Their social and political organisation was based on the patriarchal family. The tribes were ruled by kings, and the clans united under them for fighting purposes. The king was guided by the assembly of the people, called the *samiti* or *sabhā*. The people for the most part led a pastoral life, although they were beginning to show much interest in agriculture.

From the north-west of India the Āryans migrated eastwards and southwards, mainly along the river routes, and before long spread over the whole of India north of the Vindhya Mountains. Signs of their settlements farther south are seen in the Āryan names of almost all the larger rivers of South India, the Mahānadī, the Kṛishṇā, the Godāvarī, and the Tāmraparṇī.

The Āryans who settled down in Ceylon came no doubt from India, but again we are not sure from which part of that country they came. So far the study of ancient Indian dialects and of Siṅhalese has not sufficiently advanced for any definite conclusion to be reached as to which Indian dialect Siṅhalese is most closely allied to.[1] The Āryan settlers probably came about 500 B.C., from the west and the east of India, by boats that travelled along the coast and went up the rivers to the interior of Ceylon. The earliest evidence of their settlements is inscriptions in an Āryan dialect, from which modern Siṅhalese developed; and these show that before the beginning of the Christian era they had occupied the northern, south-eastern, and the eastern parts of the island. Few settled on the western and the south-western coasts. But some occupied Kälaniya and went into the interior along the river. The Āryans, with their iron weapons, must have easily driven from these parts the Väddas, who still used weapons of stone. There is no evidence of the Väddas having passed through a Copper or Bronze Age, and they could not have been a match to the Āryans, who had already entered upon the Iron Age.

The Āryans, whose chief occupation now was agriculture, led a settled life. They had some control over the supply of their food, and this afforded them some security. The leisure which agricultural activities always provide gave them a

[1] Old Siṅhalese, or Eḷu, is closely akin to Vedic, the earliest form of Sanskrit. The chief difference from Sanskrit lies in the shortening of long vowels, the de-aspiration of consonants (Sanskrit, *bhāriyā*; Pāli, *bhariyā*; Siṅhalese, *bariya*), the reduction of double consonants into single ones (Sanskrit, *Dharmarakshita*; Pali, *Dhammarakkhita*; Siṅhalese, *Damarakita*), the omission of nasals (Sanskrit and Pāli, *saṅgha*; Siṅhalese, *saga*), and the change of *s* into *h*. Such modifications are found also in other Āryan dialects of India, such as Pāli, but they have been carried to the greatest extent in the Siṅhalese language.

chance to lead a social life, to improve their minds, and to satisfy their spiritual needs.

17. *The Connection of Language with Race.* All this, however, does not prove that the Āryans who came to Ceylon are necessarily the descendants of the original Indo-Europeans. Similarity of language is not sufficient evidence to establish a connection by blood. The Väddas, for instance, speak a dialect of Siṅhalese, yet they clearly belong to a different racial stock. No one will try to prove that all the North Indians originally belonged to the same racial group because they all speak Āryan languages. The free use of English in Ceylon today shows not only that the language of a more progressive civilisation can grow at the expense of others which have not kept pace with the times, but also that those whose chief medium of expression is English need not be Englishmen.

The *Mahāvaṅsa* gives the names of a number of tribes that inhabited Ceylon. They are Siṅhala (lion), Taraccha (hyena), Lambakaṇṇa (hare or goat), Balibhōjaka (crow), Moriya (peacock), and Kuliṅga (fork-tailed shrike). All these names perhaps show that the early tribes of Ceylon were people who took their clan names from totems, or emblems, of animals or birds which they worshipped. The Siṅhala tribe probably formed the most influential clan, and gradually gave its name to the people as a whole and then to the island, just as the Angles gave their name to the people of England and to the country Engle-land.[1]

18. *The Āryan Contribution.* The coming of the Āryans was the beginning of an important stage in the history of Ceylon. Few people influenced the course of history in this island as these early Āryan adventurers did. Siṅhalese, the

[1] The modern name of the island, Ceylon, and the name given to it by the Arabs, Serendib, are only modifications of the old name, Siṅhaladīpa, the island of the Siṅhalese.

language they introduced, is still the most widely spoken in Ceylon. No other metal has yet taken the place of iron. Agriculture, which they introduced, is even today the main occupation of the people, and at that time it prepared the way for the spread of Buddhism, which, in spite of the many vicissitudes it has gone through, is yet the religion of the majority of the people of Ceylon.

19. *The Dravidians.* Besides the Väddas and the Āryans another stock of people helped to form the Siṅhalese race. There is no evidence to show when the Dravidians first came to this island, but they undoubtedly came to Ceylon from the earliest times, either as invaders or immigrants. Most of them gradually adopted the Siṅhalese language, as some of them still do in some of the coastal districts, and got merged in the Siṅhalese population.

The word 'Dravidian' does not represent a distinct race, but, like the word 'Āryan,' is a convenient label to designate those who speak Dravidian languages, such as Tamil, Malayālam, Kanarese or Telugu. The Dravidians of today are a mixture of the original Dravidians and the aborigines of India.

At the time the Āryans entered India the Dravidians were occupying not only South India but also the greater part of North India, but there is no definite evidence to show from where they came to these regions. The existence even up to the present day in Baluchistān of Brāhūi, a form of Dravidian speech, perhaps shows that the Dravidians, like the Āryans, entered India from the north-west. There is some similarity in the racial type between the Dravidians and the Sumerians, who occupied Babylonia between 4000 and 2000 B.C. Therefore, some scholars hold the view that the Dravidians are descended from these Sumerians.

20. *The Dravidian Influence on Ceylon.* Though there is sufficient evidence to prove that in the early centuries of the Christian era the Dravidians helped to form the Siṅhalese

race, nothing has yet been discovered to show that during that time they made any noteworthy contribution to the civilisation of Ceylon. Evidence of any definite cultural influence is available only after the invasions of the Pallavas, in the sixth and the seventh centuries A.D. The Dravidian influence became considerable after the invasions and occupation of Ceylon by the Chōḷians, and it grew stronger with the Pāṇḍyan invasions. The power of the Dravidians in Ceylon reached its zenith in the fourteenth century, when the Jaffna kingdom exacted tribute even from the south. The Dravidians exercised their cultural influence mainly through Hinduism, which not only became firmly established in the eleventh century, but also influenced Buddhism to a considerable extent in the succeeding centuries.

II. Buddhism and Its Introduction to Ceylon

21. *The Religion of the Early Āryans.* There is no satisfactory evidence to give us any idea of the religion of the early Āryan settlers of Ceylon, but by the time that definite evidence is available (i.e., by the first century B.C.) Buddhism had spread into every part they occupied.

The rise of Buddhism was preceded in India by many centuries of religious development. The Āryan, according to the *Rigveda*, had a very simple religion when he lived in North-West India. He worshipped the phenomena of nature, which he treated as living beings and represented in human form. He called the sky god Varuṇa, and associated with him the idea of order, both in the universe and in the sphere of morality. The thunderstorm, which caused the rain to pour, was to him the god Indra. He personified the sun as Vishṇu; and Śiva, his later rival, was at this time called Rudra, and was no more than a storm-god. The early Āryans also worshipped a few abstract deities, like Sraddhā, faith.

The literary works that followed the Rigveda, such as the

Brāhmaṇas, the commentaries on the Veda, and philosophical works like the *Upanishads*, give some idea of the life of the Āryans as they spread over the Ganges valley. They reveal a remarkable development in their religious practices and philosophical ideas. The priestly ritual had become elaborate, and animal sacrifices common.

22. *Buddhism.* Buddhism arose in the sixth century B.C., partly as a reaction against Brāhmanism, which emphasised ritual and sacrifice as a means of salvation. It objected also to the observance of caste and extreme forms of self-mortification. The Buddha accepted pain as a fact of existence, and attributed it to *tanhā*, or craving. This pain, according to him, has to be overcome by the noble eight-fold path, which consists in right views, right thoughts, right speech, right action, right means of livelihood, right endeavour, right mindfulness and right concentration. In other words, salvation according to Buddhism is attained by self-culture, which ends in the attainment of *arahatship*. A Buddhist, in order to attain this state free from passions, has to follow the *sīla*, or moral precepts, and devote himself to meditation or contemplation on virtuous things and other suitable objects.

This does not mean that the Buddhists put all emphasis on the teaching and the practices, and ignored the founder of their religion. From the very beginning they showed him great respect and devotion. In early days, when no images were used, they paid their homage to Bo-trees, under one of which he is said to have reached enlightenment, and to the *dāgābas* which were believed to contain his relics.

The Buddhists have displayed much interest also in the stories of the previous lives of the Buddha. As a *bōdhisattva* i.e. a being destined to be a Buddha, Gautama did not seek so much his own release from pain as the welfare of others. He gave up *nirvāṇa*, and by sacrificing himself for the sake of others, prepared himself for Buddhahood.

23. *The Coming of Buddhism from India to Ceylon.* The spread of Buddhism at first was due mainly to the *Saṅgha*, the order of *bhikkhus* or monks, which the Buddha established before he died. The *bhikkhus* led a life of celibacy and poverty, and depended for their food and clothing on the alms of the faithful. They handed down the *dhamma*, the teaching of the Buddha, and spread it in a few centuries through many countries of Asia.

The first home of Buddhism was in Magadha, the capital of which was Rājagaha, which stood between modern Patna and Buddh Gayā. From there Buddhism gradually spread westward along the well-known routes, and before long became well established in Avanti, the region to the north of the river Narbadā, and in regions as far off as Kashmir in the north-west. As Buddhism spread and grew, the *Saṅgha*, owing to differences of opinion, divided themselves into various schools, some of which were the Mahāsaṅghikas, the Thēravādins, the Śarvastivādins, and the Mahiśāsakas. The chief centres of the Thēravādins in the early days were Kōsambī, on the river Jamna near modern Allahābād, and the district of Avanti, of which Ujjain was the chief town. Vidisā, near which so many Buddhist monuments are yet to be found, was also not far from here.

In the time of Aśōka (274–237 B.C.), the grandson of Chandragupta Maurya (Moriya), the monarch who practically brought the whole of North India under his rule, Buddhist missionary activity received a great impetus. The peaceful conditions that prevailed throughout India during the greater part of his reign, the growth of Indian trade with foreign countries, the diplomatic missions that Aśōka sent out, and the favour shown by Aśōka himself to Buddhism after he became a convert—all this undoubtedly led to the wider spread of Buddhism. Buddhist missionaries went to many countries of Asia, and a few that belonged to the Thēravāda

School came to Ceylon, led by Mahindạ, and were favourably received by Dēvānaṅpiya Tissa, who ruled at Anurādhapura.

24. *The Pāli Language and Literature*. The Thēravāda Sect was responsible for the introduction into Ceylon of a new language and a literature. The scriptures which they used, known as the Pāli Canon, consisted of a large number of books, and they were composed in a mixed Āryan dialect which was later called Pāli. The Pāli language is rich in expression, and in medieval times the *bhikkhus* of Ceylon made use of it to write their books, just as the Christian monks of the west employed Latin. Siṅhalese, which is akin to this language, is indebted to Pāli for many of its ethical, psychological and philosophical terms.

The Pāli Canon is also called the *Tipiṭaka*, or the three baskets, as it is divided into three sections—the *Vinaya*, the rules of discipline for the *bhikkhus*; the *Dhamma* or *Sutta*, the discourses of the Buddha and some of his disciples; and the *Abhidhamma*, which deals with the philosophy of Buddhism. The *Dhamma* is divided again into five collections—the *Dīgha Nikāya*, the *Majjhima Nikāya*, the *Saṅyutta Nikāya*, the *Aṅguttara Nikāya*, and the *Khuddaka Nikāya*. Some of these books are in verse and some in prose, while others contain both prose and verse. The *Jātaka*, which is one of the books of the *Khuddaka Nikāya*, along with its commentary, consists of tales dealing with the life of the Buddha in his previous births, and the introduction in the *Jātaka* commentary is an expanded account of another book of the *Khuddaka Nikāya*, called the *Buddhavaṅsa*, or the history of the Buddha. The *Jātakas* with their moral lessons have always been popular among the Siṅhalese people. Many of the Pāli and Siṅhalese literary works begin with an account of the life of the Buddha, including his activities as a *bōdhisattva*, and many of the *Jātaka* stories have been chosen by Siṅhalese poets as subjects of their poems.

25. *The Art of Writing*. The art of writing also came to Ceylon along with Buddhism. The characters in the earliest inscriptions of Ceylon, which are yet to be seen above or below the drip ledges of caves, and from which the modern Siṅhalese script developed, are almost the same as the Brāhmī script in the inscriptions of Aśōka.

The Brāhmī script is the parent of all modern Indian alphabets, including Tamil. It shows some similarity to the Phœnician type of writing, which has been discovered in an inscription in Palestine of one Mesha, a king of Moab, who recorded his successful revolt against the Kingdom of Israel. The Siṅhalese alphabet, therefore, like the modern European alphabets, has to be traced ultimately to a Semitic origin, or to some other script from which Semitic writing was also derived. Further evidence of this connection is to be seen in some of the earliest Siṅhalese inscriptions, which are written like Arabic from right to left.

Many countries had to go through a laborious process before they developed their alphabets. Ceylon was fortunate in getting through the *bhikkhus* an alphabet sufficiently developed to express all the different sounds in the Siṅhalese language.[1]

26. *Architecture and Sculpture*. Siṅhalese brick and stone architecture and sculpture also first appeared after the introduction of Buddhism into Ceylon. The early sculptures represent events in the history of Buddhism, while the earliest

[1] The art of writing began with rough pictures of the things the people wanted to represent. The Väddas, for instance, never went beyond this stage. Next a symbol was substituted for the full picture, as in Chinese writing. In the third stage, as in the Siṅhalese alphabet, the symbol came to be used not for the thing but for the sound. This simplified the art of writing; for otherwise, as in China, the student would have to learn hundreds of symbols in order to express his thoughts in writing.

buildings, *dāgābas* and *vihāras*, were set up for the glory of Buddhism.

27. *The Influence of Buddhism on Ceylon.* Buddhism exercised its influence on Ceylon also in other ways. At a time when life was still barbarous and the opportunities for a life of culture were few, it provided the people with a moral code which served them as a guide and with religious practices which helped them to lead a disciplined life. It continued to be the main cultural influence till the arrival of the Portuguese, and by keeping up the contact between India and Ceylon, helped this island to benefit by the social and cultural movements of the sub-continent.

MAP OF ANCIENT
CEYLON

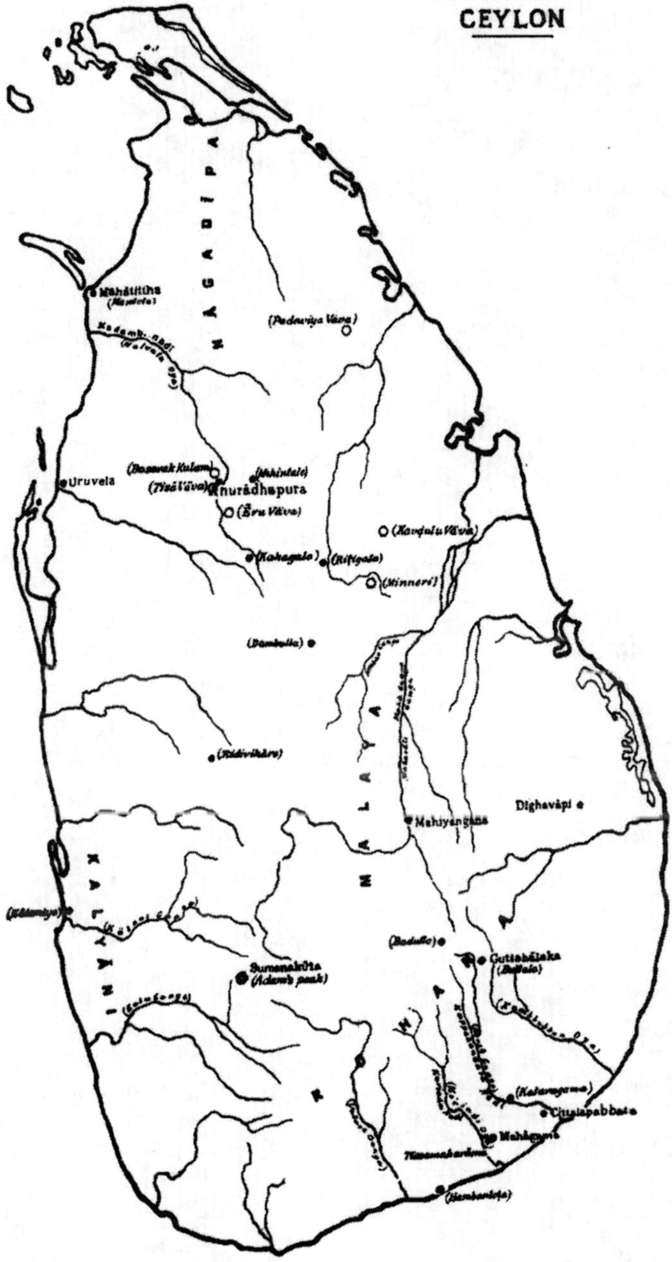

CHAPTER III

THE ANCIENT PERIOD

28. *Dēvānaṁpiya Tissa to Mahasen.* It is only after the advent of Buddhism that we are able to take up any connected story of the events of the history of Ceylon. The Ancient Period may, therefore, be said to begin with Dēvānaṁpiya Tissa, the contemporary of Aśōka (274–237 B.C.). It is marked by two features—the spread of agriculture and irrigation and the advancement of Buddhism. It ends with the reign of Mahasen (A.D. 334–362), the greatest builder of tanks and the first king to work against the Thēravāda community at the Mahāvihāra and to support sects that opposed them.

29. *The Early Settlements.* At the beginning of this period there were three main settlements or centres of population in Ceylon. The chief of these was the northern plain, with Anurādhapura as its capital. The next in importance was Ruhuṇa, the south-eastern part, the capital of which was Māgama. The third was the region watered by the Kälani Gaṅga, with Kalyāni, or Kälaniya, as its capital. Probably these three regions were independently occupied.

In the northern region, access into the interior was along the three main rivers, and the sources of these were not far from each other. Anurādhapura became the capital, both on account of its central position, near the sources of these rivers, and because of its strategic position on the Malvatu Oya, along which, after landing at Mantota, near Mannar, the invaders from South India came into the interior.

The southern settlements were mainly along the four

rivers—the Valavē Gaṅga, the Kirindi Oya, the Mänik Gaṅga, and the Kumbukkan Oya. These rivers, like those of the north, gave an opportunity for agricultural activity.

The northern plain and the south-eastern region were connected from the earliest times on account of the Mahaväli Gaṅga. The sources of the three northern rivers were not very far from the Kacchaka Ford, which was near the junction of the Mahaväli Gaṅga and its tributary, the Amban Gaṅga. There was also a definite route from Anurādhapura to this place, past Kahagala and Riṭigala. From the Kacchaka Ford one could go to Mahiyaṅgana (the modern Alutnuvara) along the Mahaväli Gaṅga, and then to Buttala, which lay near the Mänik Gaṅga.

Of the settlements around the Kälani Gaṅga there is very little information to be gathered from the chronicles or from inscriptions, and this region does not seem to have come under the influence of the kings of Anurādhapura. Owing to the heavy rainfall, it must have been thickly wooded and difficult of access either from the north or the south-east. The rivers of this region also afforded no route, as they flow from east to west. Kälaniya was an important port and was visited by foreign merchants who came in search of precious stones.

The central highlands, called the Malaya country, was very little occupied at this time by the Āryan settlers, as it was difficult of access and unsuitable for the cultivation of rice.

30. *The System of Government.* The three regions of the north, the south-east and the west of Ceylon were ruled at the beginning of the period by independent kings, under whom a number of petty rājās or chiefs ruled the different districts. At the end of the second century B.C., Duṭugämunu[1]

[1] Duṭugämunu's title, Gämuṇu, or Gāmaṇī (village chief), which was adopted also by his successors, perhaps shows that his ancestors, if not he himself, were at one time village chiefs.

(101–77 B.C.), who was ruling Ruhuṇa from his capital, Māgama, became the chief ruler of the northern and the south-eastern parts, by subduing many petty rājās and the Tamil king, Eḷāra, who ruled at Anurādhapura. He was followed by his brother, Saddhā Tissa, for the custom was that the succession should follow from brother to brother and then to their sons. Saddhā Tissa's son, Vaḷagambā, was driven out of power by five Tamils, who occupied the throne in turn. There were also other usurpers during this period. Subha (A.D. 120–126) seized the throne from Yasalālaka Tissa (A.D. 112–120). He was followed by Vasabha (A.D. 127–171), a member of the Lambakaṇṇa clan. The succession was again broken by Saṅghatissa (A.D. 303–307), a Lambakaṇṇa, who usurped the throne from Vijayakumāra shortly after his accession.

The system of government at this time was a kind of feudalism. The king received from the people a share of the agricultural produce, besides rates charged for the use of the water of the tanks; and he in turn protected them and helped them to develop agriculture. Sometimes he gave a part of his income to chiefs, and sometimes set apart a portion of it for the maintenance of *vihāras* and the provision of food for *bhikkhus*.

This form of government greatly assisted the progress of civilisation. In the hunting and pastoral stages, though the members of a tribe were more or less equals, the general poverty hindered any advance. In the agricultural stage, too, men were generally poor, but the kings and the chieftains, who accumulated wealth, used it to encourage arts and crafts. They also endowed *vihāras* and thereby helped the *bhikkhus* to use their leisure for literary and educational activities. The organisation of armies for national defence, the construction of tanks, the building of *dāgābas* and *vihāras*, the establishment of libraries, the utilising of rocks as fortresses, and the fortifying of towns with walls and moats are a result of this system of government.

31. *Agriculture and Irrigation.* The Āryan settlers appear to have taken seriously to their agricultural activities from the very beginning. They first used the water of the rivers, but when their numbers increased, and they found the rivers insufficient to irrigate their fields, they began to build tanks to collect the water and to carry on the cultivation of rice on a bigger scale.

In the flat parts of South India, water in early times was collected in shallow tanks made by digging up the soil. In other countries irrigation was carried on mainly by diverting the water of rivers into fresh channels. But in Ceylon during this period, irrigation was carried on mainly by converting shallow valleys, down which seasonal streams flowed, into tanks by the building of bunds or dams.

The earliest tanks were built in Anurādhapura, where the population increased most quickly. The Abhayaväva (now called the Basavakkulam), the Tisāväva and the Nuvaraväva were three of the first to be constructed. Vasabha (A.D. 127–171) is credited with eleven tanks and one channel. One of these is identified with Ēruväva, to the south-east of Anurādhapura. Deṭu Tis I (Jeṭṭha Tissa) (A.D. 323–334) is said to have built six tanks, and his brother Mahasen (A.D. 334–362) seventeen. One of these seventeen is identified with Kavḍuluväva and another is the Minnēriya Tank, which when full covers 4,560 acres. The tanks built by Vasabha and Mahasen must have led to great progress in agriculture and an increase of population in the region between Anurādhapura and the Mahaväli Gaṅga. And the people who benefited by the Minnēriya Tank began before long to worship Mahasen as a god.

32. *Early Schisms in Buddhism.* Buddhism, too, made great advances along with the spread of agriculture, but the

THE MINNERIYA TANK

(*Page 26*)

THE ABHAYAGIRI DĀGABA, ANURĀDHAPURA

(See page 29)

Thēravāda sect did not have everything their own way for long. In the time of Vaḷagambā, the Dhammaruci Sect arose, separated from the Thēravāda, and occupied the Abhayagiri Vihāra. In the time of Goḷu Abā (Gōṭhābhaya) (A.D. 309–323) the Sāgalika Sect came into existence. They seceded and lived in the Dakkhiṇa Vihāra, the *dāgäba* of which is the so-called Eḷāra's tomb. Both the Dhammarucis and the Sāgalikas separated because they disagreed with the Thēravādins regarding certain rules of discipline.

Divisions also took place owing to the advent of *bhikkhus* from India. Vēra Tissa (Vohārika Tissa) (A.D. 269–291) and Goḷu Abā are said to have suppressed the Vaituliyan heresy. The Vaituliyans were most probably Mahāyānists,[1] who differed from the Thēravādins (who are also called Hīnayānists) on matters of doctrine. A *bhikkhu* from Chōḷa, called Saṅghamitta, who was versed in the teachings concerning the exorcism of spirits and who had visited Ceylon in the time of Goḷu Abā, came again in the time of Mahasen, and induced the king to cease from supporting the Mahāvihāra *bhikkhus* on the ground that they did not teach the right rules of discipline.

The spread of these new teachings meant that the literature of other Buddhist schools and of the languages in which they were written came to be studied. The Mahāyānist literature was in a form of mixed Sanskrit, and its study led to some knowledge of Sanskrit, which later considerably influenced the Siṅhalese language and literature.

33. *Other Religions.* Religions other than Buddhism also existed at this time. Nigaṇṭhas and Ājīvakas are said to have lived in Anurādhapura. Of these, the Nigaṇṭhas, better known as Jains, were the followers of Mahāvīra, a religious

[1] Paranavitāna, 'Mahāyānism in Ceylon' (*Ceylon Journal of Science*, G. Vol. II, p. 35).

teacher contemporary with the Buddha. The Ājīvakas were a sect founded by Makkhali Gosāla, another teacher who lived about the same time. The common people kept up also the old religious cults. They continued to propitiate evil spirits and to worship natural objects such as trees.

34. *Architecture and Sculpture.* The Buddhist *bhikkhus* who came to Ceylon lived at first in stone caves, such as those at Mihintalē, Vessagiriya and Issurumuniya, and in groves such as the Mahāmēghavana. Not long after their arrival the *dāgäba*, now called the Thūpārāma, was built, and the Bo-tree, which still exists to the south of Anurādhapura, was planted.

After the first century A.D. the use of caves for residential purposes went out of fashion, as from the first century B.C., both in the north and the south-east, *vihāras* began to be built. The most famous of the ancient *vihāras* were the Mahāvihāra and the Abhayagiri Vihāra in Anurādhapura. The Mahāvihāra, which became famous for its literary activity, was also the great centre of orthodoxy, while the Abhayagiri Vihāra was generally associated with heretical beliefs.

These and other *vihāras*, built in the early centuries of the Christian era, had foundations of stone, as many of the remains at Anurādhapura show, while the upper parts were made of brick, wood, or clay. The other buildings of the *vihāra* included the refectory and the *upōsathaghara* (*upōsatha* house). At the latter the *Saṅgha* assembled on *pōya* or *upōsatha* days to recite the formula of the confessional. The best-known example of an *upōsathaghara* is the Brazen Palace; but its stone pillars, which still exist, may not belong to this period.

Usually every *vihāra* had also a *dāgäba* within its premises. The best known of the *dāgäbas* of this period is the Ruvanväli Säya in Anurādhapura. Iḷa Nāga (A.D. 96–103) built the *dāgäba* at Tissamahārāma in the south. Gajabā (A.D. 174–196) enlarged the Abhayagiri Dāgäba, which thus became the largest built during this period, and larger than the third pyramid of Ghizeh. The Jētavanārāma and its *dāgāba* are said to have been built by Mahasen. Thus the largest *dāgābas* were built in Anurādhapura, Kälaniya, and Tissa-mahārāma, which were the seats of kings or sub-kings, and are an index to the wealth of the kings as well as to their ability to organise labour.

The *dāgābas*, also called *cetiyas* or *thūpas*, are of pre-Buddhistic origin. They were of various shapes. The Thūpārāma Dāgäba originally was in the shape of a heap of paddy. The later ones of this period were generally built in the shape of a hemisphere. They were generally built on a round or square platform, and at the base of each there were three terraces. On the topmost of these rose the hemispherical dome. Above the dome was a square, called the *devatā koṭuwa* or *haras koṭuva*, on which stood the spire. Originally the spire was in the shape of an umbrella standing on a stone shaft. Most of the *dāgābas* of this period were of the same pattern as those at Sāñchī in Central India.

So far no traces have been discovered of buildings of this time used by laymen. The people probably lived in caves or dwellings made of destructible material. The only non-religious structure mentioned in the *Mahāvaṅsa* apart from the king's palace is the wall of Anurādhapura, built by Kuṭakaṇṇa Tissa (A.D. 16–38) and raised by Vasabha (A.D. 127–171).

There was also a certain amount of activity in sculpture during this period. The examples extant are carved on limestone, and they belong to the style of the sculptures at Amarāvatī on the river Kṛishṇā in South India.

35. *North India and the Deccan.* The country that influenced Ceylon most during this period was India, and it is not possible to understand the history of this island without

a knowledge at least of the most important events that took place in that sub-continent.[1]

Reference has already been made to the influence of North India and the Deccan on Buddhism, the architecture, and the sculpture of the island. This influence came mainly through Ceylon's contact with the Andhra kingdom (the modern Telugu country on the east coast). In the time of the Emperor Aśōka the Andhrās occupied Teliṅgāna, the region between the Gōdāvarī and the Kṛishṇā. After his death, the Andhra rulers extended their kingdom westward along these rivers and then northwards. They occupied Ujjain in the second century B.C., and Vidisā in the next century. Their capital at first was Dhānyakaṭaka, or Amarāvatī, but it was changed in the first century B.C. to a more central town, Pratishṭhāna, the moderṅ Paithān.

The principal religion of the Andhrās was Buddhism, and the Andhra kings gave it every encouragement. The widespread activities of Buddhism of this period are still to be seen in the remains of *dāgābas* and sculptures at Sāñchī, Amarāvatī, and Nāgārjunikoṇḍa on the river Kṛishṇā, and the famous halls cut out of the rocks at Kārle, Nāsik and Ajanta in Western India. Nāgārjuna, the great Mahāyānist teacher, who lived in the latter part of the second century A.D. and gave the Mahāyānist doctrines a definite form, was

[1] The political divisions of India at the period now under consideration consisted of three main regions. The most important of the three consisted of the plains in the north watered by the Indus and the Ganges. The second in importance was the Deccan Plateau, lying to the south of the Narbadā and the Vindhya mountains and to the north of the Kṛishṇā and the Tungabhadra rivers. The western half of it formed the ancient Mahārāshṭra, and the eastern half Teliṅgāna, with Kaliṅga on its north. The third region, which was generally called South India, lay to the south of the Kṛishṇā and the Tungabhadra, and consisted of the three Tamil States of Chōḷa, Pāṇḍya, and Chēra.

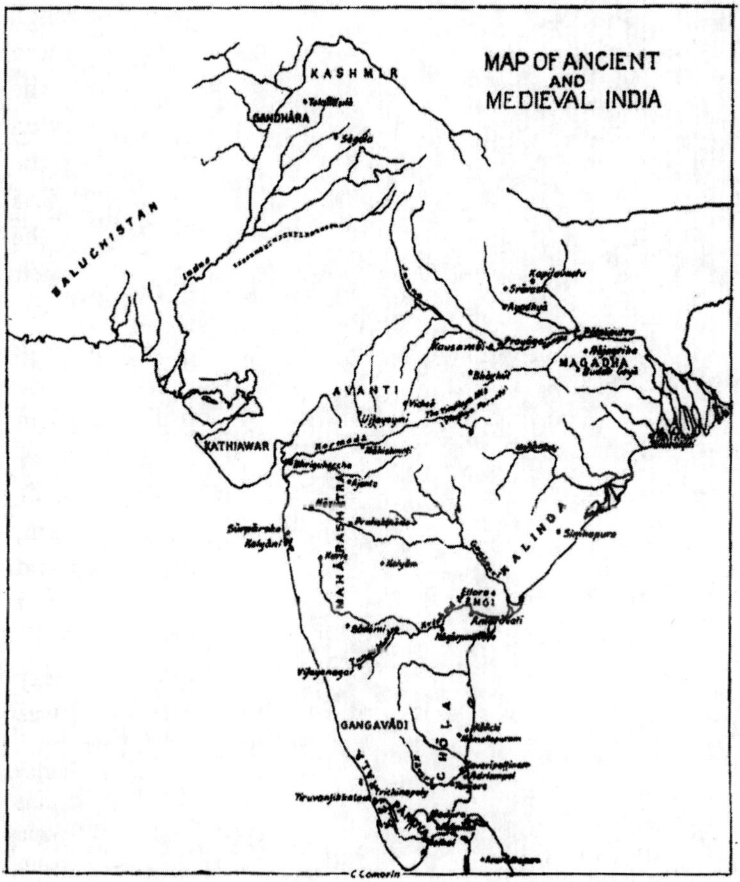
MAP OF ANCIENT AND MEDIEVAL INDIA
KASHMIR
GANDHĀRA
BALUCHISTAN
Indus
Kapilavastu
Ayodhyā
Kausambi
MAGADHA
Bhārhut
AVANTI
Ujjayini
KATHIAWAR
Narmadā
Bhrigukaccha
Ajanta
MAHĀRASHTRA
Sūrpāraka
Simhapura
KALINDA
Ellora
VENGI
Amarāvati
Bādāmi
Vijayanagar
GANGAVĀDI
CHŌLA
Kāñchi
Mamallapuram
Trichinopoly
Tiruvanjikkalam
Tanjore
Madura
PĀNDYA
C Comorin

a native of the Andhra kingdom, and Nāgārjunikoṇḍa was probably the place in which he lived.[1]

36. *South India*. Ceylon was closely connected with South India from the earliest times, but it is not possible to trace in detail their relations during this period. The Chōḷians, the Pāṇḍyans, and the Chēras either kept no records of the activities of their ancient kings or, if they did, they are no longer extant. They have left hardly any monuments or inscriptions, on stone or copper plates, older than the seventh century A.D. The main sources for the reconstruction of the history of the period are some poems and the commentaries on them, and references made by foreign writers. But these provide very few facts which we can take as certain.

The early inhabitants of the three kingdoms of South India—Pāṇḍya, Chōḷa, and Chēra[2]—were Dravidians and

[1] Ceylon's connection with North India was maintained during this time through three well-known routes, two of which passed through the Andhra kingdom. All the three routes started from Pāṭaliputra (the modern Patna). One of these passed through Prayāga (Allahābād), Kauśambi (Kōsambī), Bharhut, Vidisā, Ujjayinī (Ujjain), Māhishmatī (Mandhāta), and Pratishṭhāna (Paithān) to the mouths of the Gōdāvarī and the Kṛishṇā, and thence to Ceylon. The second continued from Māhishmatī to the seaport of Bhṛigukaccha (Bharukaccha and modern Broach), from which people sailed southwards along the coast of Western India to Ceylon after touching at Sūrpāraka (Sopāra) in the Thāna district of the Bombay Presidency. Along the third route people travelled direct by ship across the Bay of Bengal. They started from Pāṭaliputra, went along the Ganges to Tāmralipti (Tamluk) and from there to Ceylon, along the east coast. The *bhikkhus* who came to Ceylon probably followed the first route, and the traders the second and the third. The second was the best-known at the beginning of the Christian era.

[2] Ancient Pāṇḍya included the greater part of the modern Madura and Tinnevelly districts. Its capital at first was Kolkai, on the river Tāmraparṇī, and later Madura. Chōḷa extended along the east coast from the Penner to the Vellār, and westwards as far as Coorg. Its capital at first was Uraiyūr (old Trichinopoly) and later Kāviripaṭṭi-

pre-Dravidian totemistic tribes. The ruling class consisted of the cultivators, called the Veḷir (Veḷḷālar), at the head of whom were the kings. The Pāṇḍyan kings belonged to the tribe of Māṟar. Some princes bearing the title of Paḻaiyan Māṟan ruled near Cape Comorin, and the invaders of Ceylon in the time of Vaḷagambā, two of whom bore the names of Panayamāra and Pilayamāra, may have had some connection with them. The Chōḷa kings were of the tribe of Tiraiyar. Another dynasty of the same tribe ruled at Kāñchī in the time of Karikāl Chōḷa. The Chēra kings belonged to the tribe of Vānavar. Another tribe mentioned bore the name of Mōriyar, which was also the name of an ancient tribe of Ceylon. The other well-known tribe of Ceylon, the Lambakaṇṇas, are not mentioned in early South Indian literature, but later literature shows that there was a tribe by that name at least in the twelfth century.

There is no doubt with regard to the antiquity of these kingdoms. Aśōka mentions them in his inscriptions. Buddhism and Jainism had converts in these regions before the Christian era; for caves in the Madura and the Tinnevelly districts, occupied by Buddhists and Jain *bhikkhus*, possess inscriptions in pre-Christian Brāhmī characters. Greek and Roman writers refer to them even earlier, beginning from the fourth century B.C.

37. *South Indian Trade with the West.* South India was well-known for its trade from very early times. The people who came to trade with this region first were the Arabs. Their place was taken at the beginning of the Christian era by the Greek subjects of the Roman Empire, who discovered

nam. Kāñchī (Conjeeveram) was another of its large towns. Chēra, or Kērala, consisted of modern Travancore and Cochin and the Malabar district. Its capital at first was Vañji (now Tirukarūr, on the Periyar river near Cochin) and later Tiruvañjikkalam, near the mouth of the Periyar.

that the monsoons could be made use of to carry ships from the Gulf of Aden over the high seas to India. From the time of the Roman Emperor Augustus (31 B.C.–A.D. 14) till the death of Nero in A.D. 68 there was a great demand in the Roman Empire for spices, muslins, pearls, and precious stones, and that the Greeks conveyed to Rome these articles from South India is shown by the fact that the Greek words for pepper, rice, ginger, and cinnamon are derived from Tamil words.[1] After the death of Nero the trade dwindled, but it continued till the early part of the third century. The produce of Ceylon, too, was taken at first to South India, to be sold to the Greeks there, but this trade ceased in the second century A.D., when the Greeks came direct to Ceylon for the exports of this island.

38. *Foreign Literature: Indian and Greek.* Three Indian works of this period make reference to Ceylon; the writers appear to have considered this island as a sort of fairyland occupied by *yakkhas*, or non-human beings. A *Jātaka* story calls Ceylon Tambapaṇṇi, and mentions Nāgadīpa and and Kalyāṇi. According to it Ceylon was occupied by *yakkhiṇis*, or she-demons. The *Divyāvadāna*, a Sanskrit Buddhist work of the second century A.D., calls Ceylon Tāmradvīpa, and gives an account of a merchant's son who met *yakkhiṇis* in Ceylon. The tale of Kuvēni probably grew from these two stories. The *Rāmāyaṇa*, the great Indian epic, also describes Ceylon as occupied by *yakkhas* whose king was Rāvaṇa. The name Nāgadīpa (cobra island), given to the north-west of Ceylon, probably led to the growth of the legends of the *nāgas*, who, like the *yakkhas*, according to Buddhist thought, were non-human beings.

Many Greek writers, from the time of Alexander the Great,

[1] Pepper, Gk. *πέπερι*, T. pippali; rice, Gk. *ὄρυσα*, T. ariśi; ginger, Gk. *ζιγγίβερις*, T. iñji-vēr; cinnamon, Gk. *κάρπιον*, T. karuppu or kāruppu.

have referred to Ceylon, under the name of Taprobane (Tambapaṇṇi). *The Periplus of the Erythræan Sea*, a merchant's practical guide for Indian seas, written in the first century A.D., says that pearls, precious stones, muslins and tortoise-shell were exported from Ceylon, which it calls Palæsimundu. It exaggerates the size of the island and makes it almost touch Africa. Again Ptolemy, an Egyptian Greek, who lived in the second century A.D., calls Ceylon Salice, which may be a corrupted form of Siṅhalē. According to him, the products of Ceylon were rice, ginger, honey, beryl, sapphire, gold, silver and elephants. But too much reliance cannot be placed on these accounts, as the Greeks did not have a correct knowledge of Ceylon. Still the fact that the Malaya country, Anurādhapura, and the Mahavāli Gaṅga are marked with fair accuracy in Ptolemy's map shows that in the second century A.D. the Greeks knew something of the interior of the island.

CHAPTER IV

THE EARLY MEDIEVAL PERIOD (A.D. 362–1017)

39. *Kit Siri Mevan to Mihindu V.* The Early Medieval Period began with the reign of Kit Siri Mevan (Kīrti Śrī Mēghavarṇa), the contemporary of the Indian emperor Samudragupta (A.D. 326–375), who brought Northern India under his rule, and it ended with the Chōḷian conquest of Ceylon in A.D. 1017, in the reign of the Siṅhalese king Mihindu V. We have seen that in the Ancient Period, Ceylon made advances in the government of the country, in agriculture and irrigation, in Buddhism, in architecture and sculpture, and came into direct contact with India and the West. We shall note now how, during the Early Medieval Period, Ceylon made further progress in all these directions. The chief cultural influence continued to come from North India, and the relations with South India became closer. Nevertheless, the Siṅhalese people began to develop a distinct civilisation of their own.

Sixty-six kings ruled during this time, but none of them rose to great eminence. A list of them would be of little value, except to help us to make up the chronology of this period. Most of them belonged either to the Moriya or the Lambakaṇṇa clans. Their reigns were of varying length, a few lasting even less than a year. As in the Ancient Period, the dynastic succession was not left unbroken, and the throne was often usurped by a minister, the *sēnāpati*, or commander-in-chief, or by Tamil invaders.

40. *The Geographical Divisions.* The three settlements mentioned in the last chapter became definitely recognised

divisions of the island during this time, and received distinct names. The northern region, the capital of which was Anurādhapura, was called Rājaraṭa. The country south of this, and west of the mountains, was called Dakkhiṇadēsa (Southern Country). The south-eastern region continued to be called Ruhuṇa, and the central mountainous part the Malaya country. The Rājaraṭa was further subdivided into Uttaradēsa (Northern Country), Pacchimadēsa (Western Country), and Pācīnadēsa (Eastern Country). All these regions were under the Anurādhapura kings, but Ruhuṇa seems to have come under very little actual control by them.

During this period Anurādhapura continued to be the capital of Ceylon, except during the reign of Kāśyapa I. It was a large city for those days, and contained many thoroughfares and side streets. The king had his palace there, and it was also the centre of government. The numerous shrines within it made it a place of pilgrimage and the residence of a large number of *bhikkhus*. The tanks provided the necessary water for a great deal of the agricultural activity, both within and without the city, which supported the large population that it contained. It was also a centre of trade, and many foreign merchants resided there. To look after it there was a special officer, called the *Nuvara Ladda*.

Kāśyapa I (A.D. 478–496) seized the throne after murdering his father, and was therefore afraid of being driven from power, either by his brother, who fled to India, or by the people, who disapproved of his act of parricide. For this reason he left Anurādhapura and took refuge at Sīgiriya (Sinha-giri, the Lion Rock), which he made his capital. Sīgiriya is the best example of an old rock-fortress in Ceylon. In times of danger, the kings and chiefs of Ceylon, instead of building castles as was customary in Europe, usually utilised huge rocks to protect themselves from their enemies.

Another place that came into prominence during this time

was Polonnaruva. Its strategic position against invasions from Ruhuṇa had made it important. The extension of irrigation in the country around it now made it a wealthy place. Agbō IV (Aggabōdhi) (A.D. 658–674) and Agbō VII (A.D. 766–772) occupied it temporarily, and Sēna V (A.D. 972–981) retired there when the Tamils occupied Anurādhapura.

41. *The System of Government.* The kings of this time, like those of the previous period, were despotic, and the people looked upon them as *bōdhisattvas.* They were the heads of the state, and their power was limited only by the customs and the traditions of the country. The succession was from one brother to another, and then to the son of the eldest brother and his brothers. Next to the king was the sub-king, or *yuvarāja.* He was usually the heir to the throne, and was called the *mahādipāda.* From the time of Agbō I (A.D. 568–601) the *mahādipāda* was given the government of the Dakkhiṇadēsa (Southern Country), and this region came to be known later as the Mahādipāda, or Māyā Raṭa. The Malaya country was also often ruled by a member of the royal family.

The king was assisted by civil and military officials. The most important of them was the *sēnāpati*, or commander-in-chief of the army. The post of *sēnāpati* was given to one whom the king trusted fully, and naturally it was a member of the royal family that was usually appointed. Other important posts were those of the *chattagāhaka* (the umbrella-bearer), *asiggāhaka* (the sword-bearer), and of the *mahalekha* (the chief scribe), who drafted the king's edicts.

One of the chief features of the political organisation of this time was the system of village self-government. The village communities looked after the affairs of the village and enjoyed a great deal of independence. The kings rarely interfered with them, except perhaps when the king's officials visited them annually to administer justice and to collect the king's dues. The communities in villages the revenues of which the *vihāras* enjoyed, and to which the king granted immunities, exercised even greater privileges. The king's officers could not arrest even criminals within them, but the king exercised the right to fine such villages if the criminals in them were not punished.

The system of government during this period cannot be understood unless it is realised that there was very little central control, partly owing to the lack of proper communications. The sub-kings and the chiefs, like the village communities, were rarely interfered with, as long as they remained loyal and paid the king's dues. The king's chief duty was to maintain order within and to defend the country from enemies without. His other activities included the endowment of temples, the erection of religious buildings and hospitals (which he performed as religious acts), and the building of tanks, which not only helped the people but also increased his revenue.

Therefore when kings were slain or the succession broken, the people still carried on their daily activities without hindrance, unless a rebellion was prolonged, or the country was invaded by foreign kings.

42. *Agriculture and Irrigation.* The absence of any serious interference with the activities of the people probably explains the continued progress in agriculture and irrigation during this period. The cultivation of rice was carried on with greater vigour, and rice was even exported to South India. The practice of constructing large tanks, begun towards the end of the last period, was continued during the first half of this period, when some of the largest tanks were built. At the beginning of the fifth century Upatissa I built the Tōpāväva in Polonnaruva. Dhātusēna (A.D. 460–478) built the Kalāväva by setting up a dam across the Kalā Oya. Mugalan II (Moggallāna) (A.D. 537–556) also built many tanks. The

Kurunduväva, which is either the Giant's Tank or Akattimurippu, was built by Agbō I (A.D. 568–601), who is also said to have built the Mihintalē Tank and restored the Alahāra Canal, constructed during the previous period. Agbo II (A.D. 601–611) was the builder of the Kantalai and the Giritalē Tanks. The Kalāväva and the Giant's Tank when full cover an area of 4,425 acres each, while the area of the Kantalai Tank is nearly 3,500 acres.

43. *Buddhism.* The progress in Buddhism during this period was even greater. It became more and more popular, with religious festivals, innumerable shrines, the use of images, and the regular preaching on *poya* days. Even the kings began to adopt the names of Buddha's disciples or those which had some connection with Buddhism.

At the beginning of this period, in the time of Kit Ṣiri Mevan, *the daladā*, which was believed to be a tooth of Gautama Buddha and worshipped in Kaliṅga, in India, was brought to Ceylon. It was placed in a special building, which came to be called the Daladā Māligāva. Even in those days it was taken out in procession once a year, when there was great rejoicing. The *daladā* stood as a symbol of the Buddha, and before long it became the *palladium* of the Siṅhalese kings. The possession of it was considered necessary for a king, and it was removed whenever the king changed his capital.

The different Buddhist sects, too, made great headway during this time, and there was a certain amount of rivalry among them. The Dhammaruci and the Sāgalika Sects increased in numbers, and occupied *vihāras* in Sīgiriya and Mihintalē. The Chinese writers mention that there were also at this time in Ceylon the Buddhist sects called the Mahiśāsakas and the Dharmaguptakas. Both these disagreed with those of the Thēravāda School on matters of discipline. Some of the Ceylon *bhikkhuṇis* (nuns) who went to China in order to establish an Order there, belonged to the Dharmaguptaka School. There were also Mahāsaṅghikas, who were the first to separate from the Thēravāda School.

The Mahāyānists, or the Vaituliyans, as they were called in Ceylon, also exercised much influence over this island. The Mahāyāna School arose at the beginning of the Christian era, and became predominant in India about the sixth century A.D. Its missionaries went far and wide, and extolled the *bōdhisattva* ideal in preference to the *arahat* ideal. As a result of their activities, the cult of the *bōdhisattva* became prominent at this time also in Ceylon. Many *bōdhisattva* images were made and worshipped, and some of them, such as the so-called Kushṭarajā figure at Väligama, are to be seen even today. Nātha, who is worshipped even up to the present day, was originally no other than the *bōdhisattva* Avalōkitēśvara, or Lōkēśvara Nātha, whom the Mahāyānists looked upon as the Saviour of Mankind.

One of the chief results of the spread of Mahāyāna Buddhism was the extensive study of Sanskrit, in which language its scriptures were written. A Ceylon Sanskrit inscription of the seventh century A.D. records the wish of the author to be a Buddha by the merit he has gained. Another Sanskrit inscription, which belongs to the eighth century, contains the regulations for the guidance of the *bhikkhus* and laymen living within the precincts of the Abhayagiri Vihāra in Anurādhapura, or in lands belonging to it. The Abhayagiri Vihāra was well known for its tolerance of heresies, and the inscription shows that Sanskrit must have been well known among its inmates. Later Siṅhalese works reveal a knowledge of the works of Mahāyānist Sanskrit writers, such as the *Jātakamālā* of Āryaśūra (fourth century A.D.), the grammar of Chandragōmin, and the *Bōdhicariyāvatāra* of Śantidēva (seventh century).

The study of Sanskrit, as already mentioned, had far-

THE SO-CALLED FIGURE OF THE KUSHTARAJĀ

(*Page 40*)

FIGURES OF A MAN AND A WOMAN, AT ISSURUMUNIYA, ANURĀDHAPURA

(*Page 42*)

reaching results. Sanskrit supplied the Siṅhalese language with a large number of words, and helped it to grow, deepen and expand. It gave models to writers of Siṅhalese works, and brought to Ceylon a knowledge of grammar, prosody, astronomy, phonetics, and etymology, as well as of medicine, the magic arts, music, architecture and politics.

44. *Hinduism.* The spread of Sanskrit in Ceylon at this time was due also to another cause. Hinduism, as a developed form of the Brāhmanism that existed before the rise of Buddhism, began to influence Ceylon at this time as a result of its recovery in India under the Gupta kings; and the worship of Hindu gods and the practice of Hindu rites were adopted by many people. As had long been the case with the *bhikkhus*, so now the Brāhmans were maintained by the kings. The image of the Hindu god Vishṇu, which is now at the Mahādēvalē in Kandy, is said to have been brought to Devundara (Dondra) in A.D. 790. Even earlier temples for the worship of Śiva were set up at Mantota and Trincomalie, probably by Tamil settlers.

45. *Architecture, Sculpture, and Painting.* The spread of Buddhism and the growth of prosperity led also to a great advance in architecture. The shrines erected at first during this period consisted of two platforms connected by an enormous slab. One of them formed the real shrine, while the other was used as the tom-toming hall. Later this type of building was improved upon and much grander structures were erected. The building, for instance, lying to the west of the Jētavanārāma Dāgäba, was originally a vaulted building. Its brick walls and immense doorposts of stone are yet to be seen. It has a porch (*maṇḍapa*), a nave, a communication passage, and a shrine, and resembles in some respects a Christian church. The *dāgäbas* of this period are all small in size, and the platforms on which they stand are square. Perhaps the greatest piece of work of this period was the

utilisation of the Sīgiriya Rock as a fortress. The construction of the figure of a lion out of brick, the making of the galleries and the wall around it covered with marble-like plaster, certainly display great skill.

Some of the best pieces of Ceylon sculpture also belong to this period. Most of the carving is done on gneiss, as opposed to limestone of the previous period. In the early part of this period the influence of Gupta style is to be seen in the bas-relief at Issurumuniya of a man and woman, and in other sculptures, such as the figures of seated Buddhas. The moonstone at the entrance of the so-called Queen's Pavilion, carved in hard stone, is of real artistic merit.

The frescoes of Sīgiriya are the oldest paintings worthy of note found in Ceylon. They bear a remarkable resemblance to some of the scenes in the caves at Ajanta in Western India. The figures, like those at Ajanta, are painted with great skill, and the hands, holding flowers, fruit, or musical instruments, are most gracefully rendered.

46. *Literature.* The growing interest in Buddhism led to a great deal of literary activity. At the beginning of this period, or perhaps earlier, many commentaries on the Pāli Canon were written in Siṅhalese. The chief of them was the *Mahā Aṭṭhakathā* of the Mahāvihāra. But these commentaries do not exist any longer, and we cannot be sure of their date or of their exact contents. The earliest Pāli work of this period is the *Dīpavaṅsa*, a compilation of ballads and verses dealing with the introduction of Buddhism into Ceylon and the history of Ceylon up to Mahasen. The study of Pāli and the use of it for the writing of books became more common with the arrival of Buddhaghōsa from India in the reign of Mahānāma (A.D. 409–431). He is the author of the *Visuddhi Magga* (The Path to Purity), in which he gives a restatement of Buddhist doctrine. He is also said to have translated the Siṅhalese commentaries on the canonical works

into the Pāli language. His works had a profound influence on later Buddhists, and his methods of exposition of the scriptures were followed in later times even in Burma.

The most important Pāli work of this period is the *Mahāvaṁsa*, written about the sixth century A.D. It covers the same ground as the *Dīpavaṁsa*, but gives much more matter, borrowed from the *Aṭṭhakathā*. It is an epic and a work of art, and shows the influence of Sanskrit both in language and style. The *Mahāvaṁsa* was one of the two works that most influenced later Pāli and Siṁhalese literature. The other was the *Jātaka*, with its introduction, the *Nidāna Kathā*. The *Mahābodhivaṁsa*, which shows the influence of these two works, also appeared before the end of this period.

Literary activity in Siṁhalese was much less. In the time of Buddhadāsa, at the end of the fourth century, some sections of the Pāli Canon were translated into Siṁhalese. In the time of Agbō I (A.D. 568–601) it is said that there were twelve Siṁhalese poets. Before the end of this period a Siṁhalese glossary to the *Dhammapada Aṭṭhakathā* was written. This work still exists, and is called the *Dampiya Aṭuva Gäṭapada*.

The form of the Siṁhalese language in the early centuries of the Christian era was not so different from other Indian Āryan dialects as now, but at the beginning of this period Siṁhalese began to take a distinctive form. The script, too, went through a change about the same time, but it began to take on its modern rounded form only at the end of this period, when the language, too, began to be strongly influenced by Pāli and Sanskrit forms.

47. *North India.* In the Ancient Period the country that influenced Ceylon most was India. Ceylon was in touch with almost all parts of it, and its influence on Ceylon in matters of religion, in sculpture and painting have already been mentioned. After the break-up of the Maurya Empire,

India was divided into a number of independent states which often waged war against one another. In the fourth century A.D., Samudragupta brought almost the whole of North India under his rule, and ushered in an era of peace and prosperity. His supremacy was generally recognised all over India, and he claimed to have received the homage of the Sinhalese. Kit Siri Mevan sent him an embassy with gifts, to obtain permission for the building of a monastery at Buddh Gayā for the use of Sinhalese pilgrims.

During the rule of Samudragupta and his successors, India was the leading power in the East. It had dealings with the Persian, Roman and Chinese emperors. Chinese pilgrims, such as Fa-Hsien and Hiuen Tsiang, visited India, and Indian sages, like Kumārajīva, went to China. It was also in this period that Farther India and Jāva came fully under Buddhist influence.

This was also a period of Hindu renaissance. The Gupta kings were worshippers of Vishṇu, though they allowed complete freedom of worship to Buddhists and Jains. They encouraged literature, science, architecture, sculpture and painting. Sanskrit became the language of the learned. The Indian epics, the *Mahābhārata* and the *Rāmāyaṇa*, and other Sanskrit works, such as the Laws of Manu and Kautiliya's *Arthaśāstra*, took their final form at this time. Kālidāsa wrote his dramas and poems, which later influenced Sinhalese literature. It was also about this time that Kumāradāsa wrote the Sanskrit poem *Jānakīharaṇa*, or the abduction of Sīta, which became popular among scholars in Ceylon. The sculpture, which exhibited extraordinary beauty of figure, dignity of pose, and restraint of treatment in detail, and the paintings, such as the frescoes of Ajanta, reached an extraordinarily high standard of excellence. The influence of India was so extensive that many Asiatic countries looked to it at this time for the sources of their inspiration.

48. *South India.* Politically, Ceylon was more closely connected with South India, but for want of proper records we cannot trace the activities of the kings of Pāṇḍya, Chōḷa and Chēra in detail. These kings often waged war with one another, and with the success or failure of each king the boundaries of his kingdom varied.

The most famous of these early rulers was the Chōḷa king, Karikāl. About the beginning of the fifth century A.D. he defeated the kings of Pāṇḍya and Chēra, and subdued the turbulent tribes, Āyar, Aravāḷar, Kurumbar, and Oḷiyar. He made Kāviripaṭṭinam his capital, and secured it against floods by raising the banks of the Kāvēri and by constructing canals.[1] Another Chōḷa king was Accuta Vikkanta, of the Kalabbha family. He lived towards the end of the fifth century, and it was in his reign that Buddhadatta wrote the *Abhidhammāvatāra*, a handbook of Buddhist metaphysics, and in Pāli verse the *Vinaya Vinicchaya*, a compendium of the rules of discipline for Buddhist *bhikkhus*. One of the Chēra kings mentioned is Senguṭṭuvan, who most probably lived in the sixth century A.D. He made Chēra the chief kingdom in South India. One of his contemporaries is said to have been Kaval, or Kayavāgu, of Ceylon.[2] Senguṭṭuvan's successor was defeated by the Pāṇḍyan king Nedunjeliyan II, who made Pāṇḍya supreme in the south at the beginning of the seventh century, or a little earlier.

49. *Early Tamil Literature.* The literature which mentions these kings helps us further to trace the social development of the people. The Aśōkan civilisation of Northern India does not seem to have affected the Tamil poets. The earliest Tamil poems also do not show the

[1] There is no reference in Indian literature to his taking any slaves from Ceylon to work on the Kāvēri embankments.

[2] This Kayavāgu has been wrongly identified with Gajabā I, who lived in the second century A.D.

influence of either Buddhism or Jainism. They describe local cults and the worship of local gods like Murugan, who later found a place in the Hindu pantheon as Śiva's son, Skanda, who is worshipped today in Ceylon at Kataragama and other places; and it is these that received the patronage of the kings. It was only in the fifth century A.D. that Jainism became prominent in Pāṇḍya and Buddhism in Chōḷa. The Āryanisation of South India took place mainly as a result of the revival of Brāhmanism and of Sanskrit, under the Gupta kings of North India. The earliest Tamil poems show very little influence of Sanskrit or of Hindu ideas. The first work that shows definite Sanskrit influence is the earliest extant Tamil grammar, called *Tolkāppiyam*, modelled on a Sanskrit grammar called *Aindra*, written by Tolkāppiyanār in the third or fourth century A.D. The famous poem, the *Kural*, by Tiruvaḷḷuvar, of about the fifth century A.D., a book of maxims in verse, is dominated by Āryan ideas and has a number of Sanskrit words. The *Chilappadigāram* (The Book of the Anklet) is in subject matter entirely original, but its epic form is borrowed from Sanskrit. Its first two cantos deal with the story of Kōvalan and his wife, Kaṇṇagi. The third canto is a later addition, and is concerned mainly with the Kaṇṇagi or the Pattini cult. The *Manimegalai* is the last of the great works of this period. It is a Buddhist epic, and probably belongs to the seventh century A.D.

The use of Sanskrit words and the adoption of the style and imagery of Sanskrit poems by Tamil poets are not the only signs of the gradual Āryanisation of South India during the fourth, the fifth and the sixth centuries. The literary works of this period also show that in the fifth and sixth centuries the Tamil gods were replaced as far as possible by Āryan gods who were similar, and that the South Indian kings, like the Ceylon kings in the ninth century, began to trace back their descent to the Āryan Solar or Lunar dynasties mentioned in the Sanskrit semi-historical works called the *Purāṇas.*[1]

50. *The Pallavas.* In the seventh century A.D., Pāṇḍya, Chōḷa, and Chēra came under the suzerainty of the Pallavas, who came from the plains of the Deccan farther north. Very little is known of the history of the Deccan from the disappearance of the Andhras, in the first half of the third century A.D., till the middle of the sixth century. At the beginning of the sixth century the chief rulers of the region were the Pallavas, and their capital was Badāmi. About the middle of the same century they were driven southwards by the Chalukya king, Pulakesin I, who became the chief ruler of the Deccan. The Pallava king Siṅhavishṇu, who lived in the last quarter of the sixth century, has left a record that he vanquished Pāṇḍya, Chōḷa, Chēra and Ceylon; but the Ceylon records do not mention an invasion by him; nor could Pāṇḍya and Chōḷa have been ever fully subdued by him, for they joined Pulakesin II (A.D. 608–642), who fought against Siṅhavishṇu's successor, Mahendravarman I. As a result of this war between Mahendravarman and Pulakesin, the Pallavas lost Vengi (the country between the deltas of the Gōdāvarī and the Kṛishṇā, and now their only territory in the Deccan) and the famous town of Kāñchī. One of Pulakesin's brothers was appointed ruler of Vengi. Those later called the Eastern Chalukyas were his descendants, who made themselves independent; and the Western Chalukyas were the successors of Pulakesin II.

The fortunes of the Pallavas, however, changed with the accession of Narasiṅhavarman (A.D. 635–668), the ablest of the Pallava kings. He defeated Pulakesin II in A.D. 742, captured Badāmi, and made the Pallavás the dominant power in South India and the Deccan. Mānavamma of Ceylon fought for

[1] For further details see P. T. Srinivasa Aiyangar, *Tamils before 600 A.D.*

him against Pulakesin, and was helped in turn by him to capture Anurādhupura.

After the death of Narasiṅhavarman the decline of the Pallavas began. In 674 they were again defeated by the Chalukyas, and Kāñchī was lost. About sixty-six years later they suffered another severe defeat at the hands of the Chalukyas. From this they never recovered, though the Chalukyas, who had been weakened by this constant warfare, were themselves overthrown in the next century by the Rāshṭṛakūṭas.

In the ninth century Pāṇḍya and Chōḷa seem to have been more or less independent. In the reign of Sēna I of Ceylon (A.D. 831–851) the Pāṇḍyans invaded Ceylon, and were supported by the Tamils who were already in the island. Sēna II (851–885) retaliated by invading Pāṇḍya in 860 A.D. and setting up a pretender on the Pāṇḍyan throne, without any interference from the Pallavas. At the end of the ninth century a combined army of the Chōḷians and the Pāṇḍyans, led by the Chōḷa king, Āditiya, defeated the Pallavas and destroyed their power.

The Pallavas did much for the advancement of religion and of architecture and sculpture. They were patrons of both Hinduism and Jainism, and the history of stone architecture in South India begins with them. Narasiṅhavarman was the founder of the town of Māmallapuram, and it was he who caused to be made there the *rathas*, small rock-shrines, each of which was cut out from a great rock boulder. The sculptures on the rocks are executed with remarkable skill, and their influence in Ceylon is to be seen in the figures of the man and the horse carved on the rock at Issurumuniya. The Gedige at Nālanda, in Ceylon, also represents the style of the Pallava buildings. It has the typical corbel, with rolls connected by a band.

51. *The Chōḷians.* After the defeat of the Pallavas by

A FRESCO AT SĪGIRIYA

(*See page 42*)

THE GEDIGĒ, NĀLANDA

(*Page 48*)

Āditiya the chief power of South India was Chōḷa. Its supremacy was, however, not accepted immediately by Pāṇḍya, and the Chōḷa king, Parāntaka, therefore made war against the Pāṇḍyans. The Siṅhalese king, Kāśyapa V (A.D. 913–923), naturally helped the weaker kingdom in order to maintain the balance of power, and thus prevented the subjugation of Pāṇḍya. Some years later Parāntaka made war against Pāṇḍya once more, and met with success. The defeated Pāṇḍyan king came to Ceylon seeking the support of Kāśyapa's successor, Dappula V (A.D. 923–934). He failed to get any help owing to internal strife in the island, and, leaving his crown in Ceylon, went to the Kērala country. In order to obtain this crown Parāntaka invaded Ceylon in the reign of Udaya III (A.D. 945–953), but had to return without subduing Ceylon, probably owing to the defeat his forces sustained in A.D. 942 at the hands of the Rāshtṛakūṭa king, Kṛishṇa III, who captured Kāñchī and Tanjōre. Udaya took this opportunity to attack the borders of the Chōḷa kingdom. A later invasion by Parāntaka II was successfully repelled by Mihindu IV (Mahinda) (A.D. 956–972). Mihindu IV married a princess of Kaliṅga. Kaliṅga at this time was also in danger of the growing Chōḷa power and this probably was the reason for the marriage alliance.

During the tenth century the Siṅhalese were able to hold their own against the Chōḷians, because Chōḷa was not very powerful at this time and had also to defend itself against the powerful Rāshtṛakūṭa kings. At the beginning of the eleventh century, when the Chōḷians became the chief power in the peninsula and were no longer in danger of the Rāshtṛakūṭas, who had been defeated in 973 by the Western Chalukya king, Tailapa II, Ceylon found itself too weak to make any formidable resistance. Rājarāja, the Great, in 1000, when there was a change of dynasty in the Western Chalukya Kingdom, occupied a part of Mysore, and won to his side the

Eastern Chalukyas by giving his support as well as his daughter to Vimalāditya, one of the claimants to the throne of Vengi. He subdued Pāṇḍya and Kērala and invaded Ceylon about 1003. At this time the Malabar mercenaries of Mihindu V had rebelled, and Mihindu had fled to Ruhuṇa, leaving Rājaraṭa in the hands of the Malabar, the Kanarese and the Siṅhalese soldiers. Mihindu was defeated and taken prisoner by Rājarāja's son, Rājendra Chōḷa I, in 1017 and deported to South India, where he died. After that Ceylon was made a province of the Chōḷa Empire, and Polonnaruva, re-named Jananāthapura, was made the capital, probably owing to its strategic position against invasions from Ruhuṇa, where the Siṅhalese remained independent.

52. *China.* Ceylon came into direct contact with a number of other countries also. One of these was China, whose common interest with Ceylon in Buddhism brought them together. Buddhism spread to China in the first century A.D., during the rule of the Han dynasty (206 B.C.–A.D. 220), and from that time Chinese pilgrims came to India to visit the holy places of Buddhism as well as to take copies of Buddhist Scriptures. One of these, Fa-Hsien, visited Ceylon about A.D. 412 and spent two years in this country. The Siṅhalese kings sent embassies, mostly of a religious character, from early in the fifth to the middle of the eighth century, when China reached the zenith of its power under the T'ang dynasty (A.D. 618–907). At this time *bhikkhus* and *bhikkhuṇis* from Ceylon visited China, the latter to establish an Order of Nuns there. From about the tenth century, during the Sung dynasty (A.D. 960–1280), Chinese junks came to this country to exchange their goods with foreign traders that came from the west.

53. *The Trade with the West.* Ceylon's trade with the west started very early. It is not certain whether the Arabs, who came before the Christian era to south-west India, had

dealings with Ceylon. From the second century till the early part of the third century, Greek traders came to this island. There was again a revival of trade after the time of Constantine (A.D. 323–377), who made Byzantium (Constantinople) the capital of the Roman Empire.[1]

Another people that came to Ceylon to trade were the Persians, who took ship from the Persian Gulf. The Persians were originally followers of Zoroaster, the great teacher still followed by the Parsees of India and Ceylon, but those who came to Ceylon were Christians who belonged to the Nestorian Sect. Just as the Mahāyānists disagreed with the Hīnayānists with regard to the personality of the Buddha, so the Nestorians differed from other Christians in their belief with regard to the personality of Christ. The Persians also traded with south-west India, and the Syrian Christian Church of Travancore goes back to their times.

The Persian trade with Ceylon ceased in the seventh century, when Persia was captured by the Muhammadans. Muhammad before his death, in A.D. 632, became ruler over all Arabia, and his successors, called the Cāliphs, within ten years of their teacher's death, conquered Syria, Egypt and Persia. Their conquest of Alexandria in A.D. 638 stopped Ceylon's direct trade with the Byzantine Empire, and this led before long to trade relations between Ceylon and Yemen, in Arabia. Before the end of the tenth century the Arabs established a trading settlement in Colombo.

[1] It was another Byzantine emperor, Justinian (A.D. 527–565), who got the immense mass of existing laws codified, and his 'Body of Civil Law' was adopted later by most of the European countries, and was introduced into Ceylon by the Dutch.

CHAPTER V

THE POLONNARUVA PERIOD

54. *From the Chōḷian Conquest to Māgha.* From the Chōḷian conquest of Ceylon till the end of the reign of Māgha of Kaliṅga, the capital of Ceylon was Polonnaruva,[1] and this period from A.D. 1017–1235 may appropriately be called the Polonnaruva Period. Two of the greatest Siṅhalese kings lived during this time. One of these, Vijayabāhu I, who commenced his career as ruler of the Malaya district, finally made Ceylon independent of the Chōḷians, and ruled over the whole island. The other, Parākramabāhu the Great, who also ruled over the whole island, made war in South India and Pegu, set up an efficient system of administration, developed agriculture by constructing extensive irrigation works, and spread Buddhism by encouraging Buddhist literature and by setting up religious buildings. This period began and ended with South Indian invasions, and Ceylon began henceforth to be influenced more and more by South India.

55. *Political History: The Period of Chōḷian Rule* (A.D. 1017–1070). The Chōḷians ruled from A.D. 1017–1070 over the Rājaraṭa and the Dakkhiṇadēsa, which at this time was bounded on the north by the Kalā Oya and on the south

[1] The choice of Polonnaruva as the capital was probably due to two reasons. As a centre of agricultural activity Polonnaruva now surpassed Anurādhapura. As it lay in a strategic position against invasions from Ruhuṇa, where the Siṅhalese continued to be independent, it was more important than Anurādhapura to the Chōḷians, who had no enemies from South India to fear. After the expulsion of the Chōḷians the Siṅhalese kings at Polonnaruva also had little trouble from South India, while they were often at war with the Ruhuṇa rulers.

by the Kalu Gaṅga. Rājendra Chōḷa I (A.D. 1017–1042) did not make any serious attempt to conquer Ruhuṇa, though he annexed Pegu, conquered Kaliṅga, and sent expeditions to the Malay Peninsula and Sumatra. His son, Rājādhirāja (A.D. 1042–1052), who was defeated by the Western Chalukya king, Someśvara, in A.D. 1052 and in whose reign the Pāṇḍyans and the Kēralas revolted, claimed to have defeated the kings of Ruhuṇa, Vikramabāhu (A.D. 1029–1041), the son of Mihindu V, Vikrama Pāṇḍya of South India (A.D. 1044–1047) and Vīra Salamēgan (Jagatpāla of Kanauj, A.D. 1047–1051) and one Śrī Vallabha Madanarāja.

Ruhuṇa, however, never came under Chōḷian rule. It suffered from a good deal of warfare at this time, owing to the Chōḷian invasions, the counter-attacks by the Siṅhalese, and the struggles between claimants to the throne. The capital of Ruhuṇa depended much on the political conditions. Kalutara, Kataragama, Tambalagama, on the upper Giṅgaṅga, and Mahānāgakula, on the lower Valavē Gaṅga were occupied by the rulers at different times.

56. *The Reign of Vijayabāhu I* (A.D. 1070–1114). The Chōḷians were finally expelled from Ceylon in A.D. 1070 by Vijayabāhu I, a member of the Siṅhalese royal family. Kitti, as Vijayabāhu was originally called, first occupied the Malaya country. Then in 1059 he became the king of Ruhuṇa by defeating Kēsadhātu Kāśyapa, the ruler, and capturing his capital, Kataragama. After this the Chōḷians, under the powerful king, Vīrarājendra, who had defeated the Chalukyas in 1062, made war on Vijayabāhu, and he to evade them retreated to the less accessible Malaya country. After the Chōḷians returned to Rājaraṭa, Vijayabāhu made Tambalagama his capital, but before long he had to leave this and retreat to Paluṭṭhagiri, in north-west Ruhuṇa, owing to an invasion by the Chōḷian army, which had been sent to subdue rebels in Rājaraṭa. He successfully repelled this attack, and then

planned to expel the Chōḷians altogether from Ceylon. He led an army in the direction of Polonnaruva, but when his general who was sent to capture Anurādhapura was defeated by the Chōḷians, he retreated to Vātagiri, or Vākirigala, in the Four Kōralēs. This place, too, he had to abandon owing to a rebellion near Buttala. But after the rebels were subdued he ruled from Tambalagama and then from Mahānāgakula.

The Chōḷian king, Vīrarājendra, died in A.D. 1069, and his son, who succeeded him, was overthrown by the Eastern Chalukya king, Kulottunga I (A.D. 1070–1118). While Chōḷa was occupied with this struggle for the throne, Vijayabāhu made another attempt to expel the Chōḷians from Ceylon. One of his armies marched from Mahānāgakula through the Dakkhiṇadēsa, and the other by the well-known route along the Mahaväli Gaṅga. These armies defeated the Chōḷians and occupied Anurādhapura and Polonnaruva. Vijayabāhu also made Polonnaruva his capital, and renamed it Vijayarājapura.

Vijayabāhu ruled as sole monarch over all Ceylon till A.D. 1114, but his reign was not altogether a peaceful one. He had to subdue rebellions in Rājaraṭa, Dakkhiṇadēsa, Malaya and Ruhuṇa. When his ambassadors, sent to the Western Chalukya king, Vikramāditiya VI, were ill-treated by the Chōḷians, he prepared to make war on Chōḷa, but he could not carry out his plans owing to a rebellion of the Vēlakkāṛas. Moreover, he was compelled by them to flee to Vākirigala once more, and remain there till he was able to re-capture Polonnaruva.

57. *The Successors of Vijayabāhu I.* After Vijayabāhu's death the unity of the Siṅhalese kingdom broke up once more. His brother Jayabāhu became king, supported by the sons of Vijayabāhu's sister, Mittā, who married a Pāṇḍyan prince. The next in succession to Jayabāhu was Vikramabāhu, the son of Vijayabāhu by the princess of Kaliṅga, and he, according to custom, should have become the *yuvarāja*

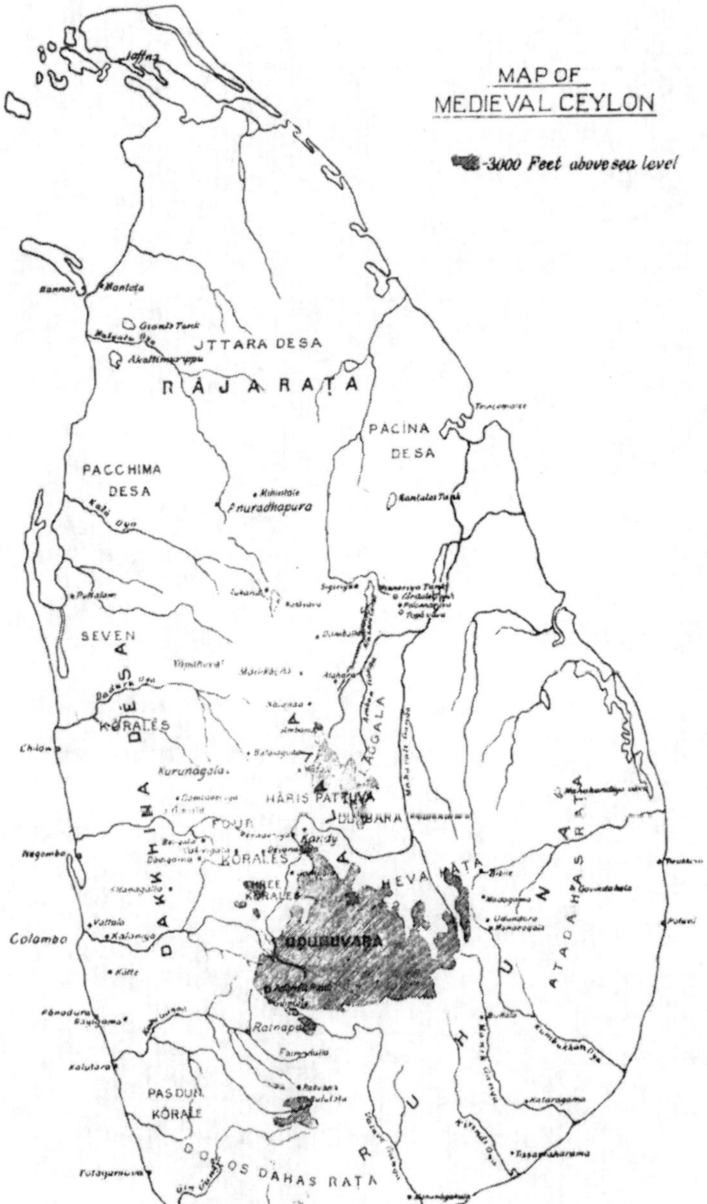
MAP OF
MEDIEVAL CEYLON
-3000 Feet above sea level
Jaffna
Mannar
Mantota
Giants Tank
UTTARA DESA
RĀJARAṬA
PACCHIMA
DESA
PACINA
DESA
Kantalai Tank
Anuradhapura
Mihintale
Trincomalee
SEVEN
KORALES
Puttalam
Chilaw
Kurunagala
HĀRIS PATTUVA
DUMBARA
FOUR
KORALES
THREE
KORALES
Kandy
Negombo
HEVA HATA
UDUBUVARA
Colombo
Kalaniya
Kotte
Ratnapura
ATADAHAS RATA
PASDUN
KORALE
DOLOS DAHAS RATA
Kalutara
Kataragama
Tissamaharama
Galle
Dondra

(sub-king) and ruler of Dakkhiṇadēsa. This place, however, was seized by Mānābharaṇa, the eldest son of Mittā, and he with his two brothers, Kīrti Śrī Mēgha and Śrī Vallabha, attacked Vikramabāhu, who was the ruler of Ruhuṇa at the time.[1] But Vikramabāhu defeated them, and, expelling Jayabāhu from the throne, became king of Rājaraṭa. Mānābharaṇa continued to rule over the Dakkhiṇadēsa from his capital, Punkhagāma, which has been identified with Dedigama, while his two brothers divided Ruhuṇa between them. Srī Vallabha ruled from Mahānāgakula the Dolosdahas Raṭa (i.e. Ruhuṇa west of the Valavē Gaṅga), and Kīrti Śrī Mēgha from Udundora (Uddhandvāra, probably Galabäda, near Monaragala), the Aṭadahas Raṭa, the eastern part.

The three brothers made a second attack against Vikramabāhu, but were defeated at Bōdhisēnapabbata and were chased towards Kälaniya. An Indian adventurer, called Vīradēva, took this opportunity to invade Ceylon. He won a victory near Mannar and marched to Polonnaruva, which he occupied. Vikramabāhu at first retreated to Koṭṭhasāra, a place which seems to have been on the other side of the Mahaväli Gaṅga, but finally defeated Vīradēva and became king of Rājaraṭa once more.

At Mānābharaṇa's death his brother Kīrti Śrī Mēgha became the *yuvarāja* and ruler of the Dakkhiṇadēsa and Srī Vallabha obtained the whole of Ruhuṇa. Vikramabāhu II died in 1137, and was succeeded by his son, Gajabāhu II. The two brothers, Kīrti Śrī Mēgha and Śrī Vallabha, made an attack against Gajabāhu too, but failed to conquer Rājaraṭa.

Vijayabāhu I — Jayabāhu — Mittā

Vijayabāhu I
- Vikramabāhu II
  - Gajabāhu II

Mittā
- Mānābharaṇa
  - Parākramabāhu I
- Kīrti Srī Mēgha
- Srī Vallabha
  - Mānābharaṇa

58. *Parākramabāhu I* (A.D. 1137–1186). A new figure now came on the scene. Parākramabāhu, the son of Mānābharaṇa, at his father's death lived at Mahānāgakula with his uncle, Srī Vallabha. After some time, however, he came to Dakkhiṇadēsa and lived with Kīrti Śrī Mēgha, who ruled from Sankhatthalī. Before long he conspired against his own uncle, and killed his uncle's general at Badalatthalī (Batalagoda). Next he defeated his uncle's supporters at Buddhagāma (Mänikdena, in the Matale district), and intrigued with Gajabāhu's general at Kalāväva. His uncle sent troops against him, but Parākramabāhu defeated them and went to live with Gajabāhu, to whom he gave his sister in marriage. But his friendship with Gajabāhu did not last long. He returned once more to Kīrti Śrī Mēgha after getting reconciled to him, and succeeded him at his death as the ruler of Dakkhiṇadēsa.

Parākramabāhu was too ambitious to be satisfied with being a ruler of only a part of Ceylon. So after making careful preparations for a war, he sent one of his generals to occupy the Malaya country. When this general had defeated the forces sent by Gajabāhu and established himself in this region Parākramabāhu started a definite campaign. One of his armies forced its way up the Kalā Oya from its mouth, and another marched from Dumbara and made its way past Bōgambara, in the Laggala district, through Ambana, into the Alahära district. A third captured Anurādhapura and occupied the city. Gajabāhu tried to get back Anurādhapura, but failed. He, however, seems to have had some success against the second army; for Parākramabāhu had to occupy the Alahära district once more before he marched to Polonnaruva from Nālanda. Gajabāhu was captured in the end, but Mānābharaṇa, the son of Srī Vallabha and cousin of Parākramabāhu, who was now ruler of Ruhuṇa, came to his aid and defeated Parākramabāhu. Mānābharaṇa treated

Gajabāhu so badly that the latter sought the help of Parākramabāhu. Then, when Parākramabāhu's general captured Polonnaruva again and set Gajabāhu free, Mānābharaṇa escaped to Ruhuṇa. Gajabāhu fought Parākramabāhu once more, and the two kings finally came to an agreement. Each retained his kingdom, but it was decided that whoever survived should succeed to the dominions of the other.

Gajabāhu died in 1153, but Parākramabāhu could not become king of Rājaraṭa at once, because Mānābharaṇa, too, wanted to succeed Gajabāhu. A war followed, and the fighting took place mainly along the Mahaväli Gaṅga, which Mānābharaṇa in vain tried to cross. Parākramabāhu made an attack also from the other side, entering Ruhuṇa from the north-west of it. Soon after he had to withdraw a part of his troops, in order to put down a rebellion raised by his general, Nārāyana. Mānābharaṇa took advantage of the situation, and crossed the river, but he was defeated by Parākramabāhu's troops. In his next attempt he was more successful. He forced Parākramabāhu to leave Polonnaruva, and pursued him towards Kälaniya. Parākramabāhu then made one more attempt to regain the throne. He defeated Mānābharaṇa's forces at Kaläväva, and, after fighting near Polonnaruva for abouts six months, defeated Mānābharaṇa, who fled to Ruhuṇa, where he died soon after.

Some of the chiefs of Ruhuṇa, however, did not accept the supremacy of Parākramabāhu. Supported by Mānābharaṇa's mother, Queen Sugalā, they rose in rebellion in 1157. An army was sent to put down this revolt, but further action was delayed owing to a mutiny of the Vēlakkāra, the Kērala and the Siṅhalese mercenaries. After this was suppressed the army sent against Ruhuṇa marched along the Mahaväli Gaṅga and fought the rebels near Bibile, Mädagama, Udundora and the Mahakaṇḍiyaväva. The *daladā* was captured, but Parākramabāhu's forces failed to pass Buttala.

Then an attack was made by Parākramabāhu, also from the west. One army marched along the coast and captured Gintota, Väligama, Devundara and Kamburugamuva. Another army went by way of Pälmaḍulla passing Rakvāṇa. After protracted fighting Sugalā was defeated and Udundora was captured. The supremacy of Parākramabāhu was challenged twice more after this. The first of the two rebellions took place in Ruhuṇa in 1160. The second occurred at Mantota. Both were easily quelled.

59. *Parākramabāhu's Successors.* Parākramabāhu was succeeded in 1186 by his nephew, Vijayabāhu II, who came from Kaliṅga. He was followed by his brother, Niśśanka Malla. They probably belonged to the Kaliṅga faction, as they tried to please those who suffered at the hands of Parākramabāhu. They were followed by nine rulers of no importance, including Parākramabāhu's queen, Līlavatī, and Niśśanka Malla's queen, Kalyānavatī, who were in turn followed by two foreign conquests. In 1211 Parākrama Pāṇḍu came from South India, deposed Līlavatī, and ruled for three years. He was deposed in turn by Māgha of Kaliṅga. During his reign of twenty-one years Māgha oppressed the *bhikkhus* and the people, and plundered their wealth.

60. *The System of Government.* The system of administration during this time did not differ much from that which existed in the preceding period. A new ministerial office came into existence, perhaps as a result of the Chōḷian influence. In the time of Kīrti Śrī Mēgha the Dakkhiṇadēsa was ruled by two *adhikarins* or *adigars*, and Parākramabāhu added a third. The government was carried on by twelve governors and eighty-four rulers of smaller districts. Parākramabāhu is also said to have reorganised the offices of state as well as the various departments.

The King's Council at this time consisted of the *yuvarāja*, the princes, the commander-in-chief, the principal chiefs, the *mahalekha*, the governors of the provinces, the chiefs of the districts, and the principal merchants. The extent of the powers of this body is not known.

61. *Warfare.* The army in Ceylon differed to some extent from the armies in India, which consisted of riders on elephants, cavalry, charioteers and foot-soldiers. In Ceylon, too, horses, chariots, and elephants were used, but they were rather the exception than the rule. This was due to the thickly-wooded nature of the country and the absence of good routes except in the east, where Niśśanka Malla set up stones every two miles. The generals travelled on palanquins, and parasols were the badge of their power.

The weapons used were bows and arrows (which were sometimes poisoned), swords, daggers, spears and clubs. Shields, made of buffalo hide, were used for defence.

The troops were mainly local levies. The mercenary soldiers, who were employed to a large extent, came from Malabar, Kanara, and other parts of South India. The *Vēlakkāṛas* belonged to a commercial corporation with a wide organisation, whose board of directors was in the Marāṭha country, but with branches in many parts, including Ceylon, with their own local assemblies. This commercial corporation was a semi-military body, and the *Vēlakkāṛas* formed some of the Chōḷa regiments. They probably came to Ceylon during the Chōḷian occupation, and they exercised much influence in the time of Vijayabāhu I and Parākramabāhu I.

Cities such as Polonnaruva were fortified with walls and trenches. Defeated armies often retreated to rock-fortresses, such as Vākirigala, where they could more safely defend themselves. Temporary fortresses were also made by driving rows of stakes like spear-points into the ground, and by digging between them ditches, in which sharpened stakes and thorns were placed. There are also references to turrets, walls, and bastions, and the building of bridges across the rivers for the transporting of troops.

The rivers formed the main routes of the armies. They were a hindrance as well as a help to conquest. The armies from the south could go along the Mahaväli Gaṅga from Alutnuvara, but they had the difficulty of crossing the river to attack the Rājaraṭa troops. Hence Polonnaruva was attacked more often by troops that marched along the northern bank of the Ambangaṅga, though this route was more difficult. The armies that marched south on the eastern side, passing Bibile, Mädagama, and Monaragala, were easily checked near Buttala, as, in order to reach it, they had to cross the Kumbukkan Oya and a mountain pass. Therefore Ruhuṇa was attacked often from the west, the armies marching along the coast or by way of Pälmaḍulla and Bulutoṭa. The Malaya country was always difficult to be conquered, owing to the dense forests and the mountainous nature of the district.

62. *Agriculture and Irrigation* There was undoubtedly a great deal of agricultural activity, in spite of the numerous wars. Vijayabāhu I repaired a large number of tanks. Parākramabāhu, when he was ruler of the Dakkhiṇadēsa, diverted the waters of the Deduru Oya for agricultural purposes by the construction of canals. He is said to have also drained the swamps in the Pasdun Kōralē. After he became king of the whole island he did even more for the advancement of agriculture. He repaired numerous tanks and built the Sea of Parākrama, by enlarging the Tōpäväva to include the modern Dumbutuluväva. He opened out a large number of canals, such as the Ākāsagaṅgā (Aṅgamädilla Ala), connecting the rivers and the tanks to make agriculture easier.

63. *Buddhism and Hinduism.* At the beginning of this period, Buddhism did not have the same vitality as in the preceding centuries The Chōḷian occupation of Ceylon for

more than fifty years gave it such a setback that Vijayabāhu I had to get *bhikkhus* from Rāmañña to renew the priestly succession. He had also to effect a purification of the *Saṅgha.* Parākramabāhu I and Niśśanka Malla also expelled unworthy *bhikkhus* from the *Saṅgha* and reconciled the three *nikāyas*, or sects. In the time of Parākramabāhu I, Buddhism once more made great progress, but at the end of this period it suffered again at the hands of Māgha of Kaliṅga, who destroyed Buddhist shrines and forced people to be Hindus.

It was also during this period that it became a common practice to make pilgrimages to Adam's Peak, in order to worship the footprint which was believed to be that of the Buddha. Vijayabāhu I provided resting-places along the route from Rājaraṭa, and set apart the village of Gilimalē, in the Ratnapura district, for the supply of food to pilgrims.

The possession of the *daladā*, which was brought to Ceylon at the beginning of the preceding period, was definitely considered an additional claim to the right of kingship, and princes fighting for the throne made it a point to capture this relic as well as the alms-bowl. One of the two religious buildings credited to Vijayabāhu I is a Tooth Relic Temple, which he got his general to build, and the protection of which, as well as the villages, the retainers, and the property belonging to it, were entrusted to the Vēlakkāṛa community.

Hinduism received a great deal of encouragement in Ceylon during the Chōḷian occupation, and its influence did not disappear with the expulsion of the Chōḷians. The Ceylon kings after Vijayabāhu I were children of princes or princesses of Pāṇḍya or Kaliṅga, and they not only kept up Hindu practices but also built Hindu temples. Hinduism also led to the greater observance of caste rules. Some kings of Ceylon are said to have followed the Laws of Manu. Vijayabāhu I built on Adam's Peak a lower terrace, from which people of the so-called lower castes could worship. Niśśanka

Malla pointed out that *Kshatriyas*, or members of a royal family, alone should be made kings and not persons of other castes.

At this time the theory of kingship in Ceylon was also further developed. In the preceding centuries a king was considered a *bōdhisattva*. According to Niśśanka Malla, an impartial king was like a Buddha; and though kings appeared in human form they were to be regarded as gods just as the Hindus looked upon their kings.

64. *Architecture, Sculpture, and Painting.* The prosperity under the Polonnaruva kings led to a great deal of activity in architecture, sculpture and painting. Once more building projects were made on a grand scale. Parākramabāhu built the largest *dāgäba* on record, the Demaḷa Maha Säya in Polonnaruva, which survives today only as a mound. The Kiri Vehera, another *dāgäba* built by him, and the Rankot Vehera, built by Niśśanka Malla, are also large in size and of hemispherical shape, like the large of *dāgäbas* of Anurādhapura.

The *vihāras* of this period were also the largest built in Ceylon, and are made of brick and lime mortar. The Thūpārāma of Polonnaruva, probably built by Vijayabāhu I, and the Laṅkatilaka and the Uttarārāma, near the Demaḷa Maha Säya, were built by Parākramabāhu. The Thūpārāma has above it a sort of dome and on its walls there is a good deal of stucco work, which shows a remarkable development in this period. These buildings are in style similar to the building to the west of the Jetavanārāma Dāgäba in Anurādhapura. In the Laṅkatilaka and the Uttarārāma Vihāras there are several fresco paintings, depicting, among others, certain *Jātaka* stories. The ruins of Parākramabāhu's palace are still to be seen, but it cannot actually have been so large as it is said to have been in the *Cūlavaṅsa*.

The influence of the Chōḷian occupation is to be seen in the architecture, too. The Chōḷa kings, who at first supported

THE KIRI VEHERA, POLONNARUVA

(*Page 62*)

THE LAṄKATILAKA VIHĀRA, POLONNARUVA

(Page 62)

Buddhism, became worshippers of Śiva in the seventh century, and they did much for the advancement of their faith by erecting temples. Rājarāja, the Great, was the builder of the large temple at Tanjore, and for the maintenance of it, the revenue of many villages, including some even in Ceylon, was set apart. The temple, known as Śiva Dēvālē No. 2, in Polonnaruva, was probably built during the Chōḷian occupation. It is entirely of stone and belongs to the eleventh century Chōḷa style. The dome of the Thūpārāma may also be due to the Chōḷian influence.

The figures carved out of the rock during this period are also large in size. The images of the Buddha at Aukana, near the Kalāväva, and at the Uttarārāma, in Polonnaruva, are some of the largest images in Ceylon. The best piece of sculpture of this period is the figure cut out of the rock near the Potgul Vehera, in Polonnaruva, and identified by some as Parākramabāhu the Great and by others as Agastya. But other pieces of sculpture in Polonnaruva, such as the moonstones, show a decline in the art. There is no longer the simplicity and the vitality of the Gupta style. On the other hand, perhaps as a result of the Dravidian influence, there is a tendency towards over-ornamentation and excessive detail.

65. *Literature.* During this period there was a good deal of literary activity, mainly due to the revival of Buddhism and the extensive study of Sanskrit works by the *bhikkhus.* The practice of writing in Pāli was kept up, and most of the books written at this time were expositions or summaries of the works of the Pāli Canon, such as the *Abhidhammatha Saṅgaha.* A number of *ṭīkās*, or sub-commentaries, were also written, explaining and supplementing the commentaries on the Pāli Canon written in the previous period.

The study of Sanskrit influenced both the Pāli and the Siṅhalese languages, as well as the choice of subjects and the form of the literary works. A few persons even attempted to write in Sanskrit. Works on Pāli prosody, rhetoric, grammar and lexicography were composed, based on Sanskrit models. The Pāli Grammar of Moggallāna, for instance, was based on the *Vyākaraṇa* of Chandragomin, and the *Abhidhānappadīpikā* on *Amara Kosha*, the Sanskrit Dictionary

The Pāli poem, *Dāṭhāvaṁsa*, a history of the tooth relic, also belongs to this period. It is in subject matter similar to the Pāli prose work, the *Mahābōdhivaṁsa*, and is written like it in a form of Sanskritised Pāli. To Dharmakīrti, the author of the *Dāṭhāvaṁsa*, is also attributed the first part of the *Cūlavaṁsa*. It is influenced to a great extent by the Sanskrit *kāvya* literature and by the rules of Indian poetics, called *alaṅkāra*. The author of the *Cūlavaṁsa* reveals a knowledge of many Sanskrit works, such as the *Arthaśāstra* of Kautiliya and the works of Kālidāsa.

Very few works were composed in Siṅhalese, as the tradition was still in favour of writing in Pāli. A few more glossaries and translations of works of the Pāli Canon were made. Towards the end of the period two important prose works and two poems came to be written. The prose works are the *Amāvatura* and the *Dharmappradīpikāva* (a commentary on the Pāli *Mahābōdhivaṁsa*), both written by Gurulugōmi. The two poems, which are the oldest extant in Siṅhalese, are the *Sasadāvata*, written at the end of the twelfth century, and the *Muvadevdāvata*. The subjects of the two poems are *Jātakas*. The *Sasadāvata* (*Sasajātaka*) deals with the story of the *Bōdhisattva* when he was born as a hare. The *Muvadevdāvata* deals with *Makhādēva Jātaka*. The form of the poems reveals a close imitation of the Sanskrit works of Kālidāsa and of his successors, like Kumāradāsa.

66. *Foreign Relations*. Ceylon had direct dealings with many foreign countries during this time. In the time of Vijayabāhu I, the foreign policy depended on the Chōḷian menace. Vijayabāhu naturally tried to be friendly with those

countries that were opposed to Chōḷa. When he was trying to free Ceylon from the Chōḷian yoke he sought the help of Rāmañña (Pegu), which had suffered at the hands of Rājendra Chōḷa I. He made alliances with Kaliṅga and Pāṇḍya, by marrying Tilokasundarī of Kaliṅga and by giving his sister, Mittā, in marriage to a Pāṇḍyan prince. He became also an ally of the Western Chalukya king, Vikramāditiya VI (A.D. 1076–1128), who was constantly at war with the Chōḷa king, Kulottunga I, who became king by expelling Vikramāditiya's brother-in-law from the throne.

When Parākramabāhu I ascended the throne there was no need for such alliances, because the Chōḷa power had declined after the death of Kulottunga. Therefore, when there arose some disagreement with Rāmañña over the trade in elephants, and when a Siṅhalese princess sent to Cambodia was seized by the king of Rāmañña, Parākramabāhu did not hesitate to declare war against Rāmañña. His fleet captured Kusumi (Bassein), and his army carried on the war for another five months until a settlement was made. After that Ceylon and Rāmañña continued to be on friendly terms. Vijayabāhu III and Niśśanka Malla had relations with Rāmañña. Niśśanka Malla claimed to have had dealings also with countries as remote from Ceylon as Rājputāna and Cambodia.

In the time of Parākramabāhu the Siṅhalese waged war also in South India. In 1167 the Pāṇḍyan king, Parākrama, whose right to the throne was contested by the Pāṇḍyan, Kulasēkhara, sought the help of Parākramabāhu against his rival. Parākramabāhu sent an army under his general, Laṅkapura who captured Rāmēśvaram and afterwards Madura. Madura then was in the possession of Kulasēkhara, who had defeated and killed Parākrama Pāṇḍya, and Laṅkapura restored the dead king's son, Vīra Pāṇḍya, to the throne. Kulasēkhara now took refuge with the Chōḷa king Rājādhirāja II, and with his help won back the throne of Pāṇḍya.

Laṅkapura was defeated, and his head was nailed to the city-gate at Madura. Kulasēkhara seems to have died soon after, for when Vīra Pāṇḍya's son, assisted by the Siṅhalese, waged war again, the king whom he drove from the throne was not Kulasēkhara, but his son Vikrama Pāṇḍya. Vikrama Pāṇḍya, like his father, sought the help of the then Chōḷa king, Kulottunga III, who sent an army, which defeated the son of Vīra Pāṇḍya, captured Madura, placed Vikrama Pāṇḍya on the throne, and drove the Siṅhalese out of India. This was the last great victory of the Chōḷians. Rāmēśvaram, which came under the rule of Ceylon during this war, continued to form a part of the Siṅhalese kingdom until the time of Niśśanka Malla, who renovated the temple there and called it Niśśankēśvara.

CHAPTER VI

THE DECLINE OF THE SIṄHALESE KINGDOM

67. *Vijayabāhu III to Parākramabāhu VIII.* This chapter deals with the history of Ceylon from the reign of Vijayabāhu III (A.D. 1232–1236) till that of Parākramabāhu VIII (A.D. 1484–1518), in whose reign the Portuguese arrived in Ceylon. The Polonnaruva Period ended with a number of invasions from South India, and the last two Polonnaruva kings were adventurers from Pāṇḍya and Kaliṅga. The pressure from South India continued during the course of this period, and the story tells of the decline of the Siṅhalese kingdom.

There were only two great kings during this period, Parākramabāhu II and Parākramabāhu VI. The former was more famous for his literary and religious activities than for his performances as a warrior or statesman. According to available evidence, though he conquered Anurādhapura and Polonnaruva, he does not appear to have ruled over the Jaffna Peninsula. Parākramabāhu VI was the greatest king of this time, and he held sway over the whole of Ceylon.

68. *The Geographical Divisions.* The main geographical divisions of Ceylon during this period were almost the same as in the preceding period; but the three divisions, or Trisiṅhala, were now called Pihiṭi Raṭa, Māyā Raṭa and Ruhuṇa. Polonnaruva no longer exercised the same influence over Ceylon as previously; and Parākramabāhu II occupied it only temporarily. Vijayabāhu IV, who made it his capital, ruled only for a couple of years. Parākramabāhu III was able to rule from there because he seems to have accepted the suzerainty of Pāṇḍya. Even when these three kings had

Polonnaruva as their capital they did not rule over the whole of Pihiṭi Raṭa. The Jaffna kings were independent rulers, and had as their capital first Sinkaı Nakarai (Siṅhanagara) and later Yāpāpaṭuna (Jaffna).

Five other towns that were the capitals of kings during this time were Dambadeniya, Yāpahuva, Kurunägala, Gampola and Kōṭṭe. The first three are rock fortresses. Gampola, like Kandy, is protected by the mountains. Kōṭṭe at this time was surrounded by marshes. The choice of such places as capitals, as that of Sīgiriya in the Early Medieval Period, shows the insecurity in which the kings of this time lived. They could no longer live in the open plains and protect their subjects, but had to seek places which gave protection to themselves. Some of the other places occupied by sub-kings and chiefs, such as 'Pērādeniya, Gandenigala, and Gōvindahela (the so-called Westminster Abbey, an imposing rock near the east coast, twenty miles west of Tirrukkovil) were also places which were protected by nature.

69. *Political History.* The unsatisfactory nature of the sources makes the history of this period somewhat obscure. It is not even easy to follow the succession of kings, owing to the lack of information about the lineage of some of them. The first Siṅhalese king of this period, Vijayabāhu III, was not related to any of the Polonnaruva kings. He and his successors added the title of 'Śrī Saṅgabo' to their names. The kings after him, till Parākramabāhu IV, were his descendants, and their rule was interrupted only during the period after Bhuvanekabāhu I, when the Pāṇḍyans seem to have ruled Ceylon. Vijayabāhu's capital was Dambadeniya, near Giriulla. His son, Parākramabāhu II (A.D.1236–1271), after the capture of Anurādhapura and Polonnaruva from the Tamils, occupied Polonnaruva for a short time. Bhuvanekabāhu I (A.D. 1273–1284) made Dambadeniya the capital once more, after the

SIVA DĒVĀLĒ No. 2, POLONNARUVA

(*See page 63*)

THE YĀPAHUVA ROCK

(*Page 68*)

assassination of his brother, Vijayabāhu IV (A.D. 1271-1273), by the commander-in-chief of the troops. He shifted the capital later to Yāpahuva, as it was easier to repel Tamil invasions from there. Vijayabāhu IV's son, Parākramabāhu III (A.D. 1302–1310), changed the capital once more to Polonnaruva, probably because he received the protection of the Pāṇḍyan king. His cousin, Bhuvanekabāhu II (A.D. 1310–1325), who defeated him, continued to rule from Kurunägala, probably because he could not get any support from the Tamils who occupied the Polonnaruva district. Bhuvanekabāhu II's son, Parākramabāhu IV, succeeded; but the lineage of the six kings who ruled after him is not known, except that Parākramabāhu V (A.D. 1348–1360) was a son of Vijayabāhu V. The third of these kings, Bhuvanekabāhu IV (A.D. 1346–1353), made Gampola his capital. It is probable that the capital was shifted from Kurunägala to Gampola owing to civil strife among the Siṅhalese themselves. It is also possible that the retreat southwards and into the interior was due to the pressure from the Jaffna Kingdom.

With Vīrabāhu II (A.D. 1391–1397), though he was connected with the royal family of Gampola, a new dynasty commenced. He continued to rule from Rayigama, east of Pānadura; most probably because he was successful over the *de facto* ruler of the time, Vīra Alakēśvara, and because he found this a better place from which he could deal with the hostilities of the Tamils and the Moors.

The succession was broken again by Vīra Alakēśvara, who seized the throne from Vīrabāhu's second son, and called himself Vijayabāhu VI (A.D. 1397–1409). He was carried away by the Chinese, and his son, Parākramabāhu VI, after killing a certain Parākrama who occupied the throne after the capture of his father, made Kōṭṭe his capital. It is not certain why the capital was shifted to Kōṭṭe. It might have been due to the growing importance of Colombo owing to the trade in spices, or merely to the protection which the marshes gave it against invasions.

The Malaya country, now called Kanda Uḍa Pas Raṭa, at this time consisted of Uḍuṇuvara, Yaṭinuvara, Hārispattuva, Hēvahäṭa and Dumbara. This region grew in importance as some kings made Gampola, within this area, their capital. When the capital was in the low-country some of the chiefs that ruled this region tried to be independent. Parākramabāhu VI (A.D. 1411–1468) had to suppress a rebellion raised by the ruler, Jotiya Siṭāno, who refused to pay tribute, and Bhuvanekabāhu VI (A.D. 1473–1480) had to bring this region once more under his rule.

70. *The Vanniyars.* Another area in which the chiefs tried to be independent was the Vanni. The Vanniyars are mentioned first during this period. They seem to have occupied the frontier country between the Jaffna and the Siṅhalese kingdoms, and acknowledged the supremacy of one of these, or remained independent whenever possible. Vijayabāhu III became king of Vanni before he expelled the Tamils from Māyā Raṭa. The Vanniyars acknowledged the supremacy of Parākramabāhu II and Vijayabāhu IV, and were entrusted with the protection of Anurādhapura by the latter They were subdued by Bhuvanekabāhu I soon after he became king. It is probable that the Vanniyars tried to be independent after the Tamil invasion, at the beginning of his reign. They seem to have been independent, or under the Jaffna kingdom later on, as Parākramabāhu VI made war on them and subdued them before the conquest of Jaffna.

71. *The Jaffna Kingdom.* Of the Jaffna kingdom it is not possible to give a continuous account. The Pāli and the Siṅhalese chronicles and almost all the inscriptions give an account only of the reigns of the Siṅhalese kings. Almost all of these rulers till Parākramabāhu VI, though they claimed to

be rulers of Trisiṅhala, did not exercise power, except during short periods, over Pihiṭi Raṭa and Ruhuṇa north of Bibilē. The northern part of Ceylon was under the Siṅhalese kings at least till the time of Parākramabāhu the Great. It is not clear when it first became an independent kingdom under the Tamils; but there is reason to think that it came into existence with Māgha of Kaliṅga, as his contemporary and successor, Vijayabāhu IV, expelled the Tamils only from Māyā Raṭa. At the beginning of the reign of Parākramabāhu II the Tamils must have been occupying both Pihiṭi Raṭa and Ruhuṇa north of Bibilē. In the time of Parākramabāhu II they lost Anurādhapura and Polonnaruva, aud about the middle of the thirteenth century they appear to have come under Pāṇḍyan rule. They regained, after the reign of Vijayabāhu IV, what they lost to Parākramabāhu II, but lost this area again in the time of Parākramabāhu III. When Bhuvanekabāhu II became king, about A.D. 1310, they seem to have got back Polonnaruva once more, and became independent of Pāṇḍya about the same time. In A.D. 1344, when Ibn Batuta, the Arab traveller, visited Ceylon, the Jaffna king was a powerful ruler, whose kingdom extended as far south as Puttalam, where the pearl fishery was under his control.

The Jaffna kings seem to have extended their power southwards during the next few decades, and exacted tribute from the Siṅhalese kingdom. To put an end to this control, Niśśanka Alagakonnāra, also called Alakēśvara, prepared for war and built fortresses at Kōṭṭe and Rayigama, east of Pānadura. At the end of the reign of Vikramabāhu III, when Alakēśvara felt that his army was strong enough to resist the Jaffna king, he defied him by hanging the Jaffna tax-collectors. The Jaffna king, Ārya Chakravarti, then sent two armies, one by sea and the other by land. The one that went by land seems to have had some success, as Bhuvanekabāhu V is said to have fled from Gampola to Rayigama. But the Tamils were finally defeated, and Alagakkonāra captured the encampments at Colombo, Vattala, Negombo and Chilaw.

In the time of Parākramabāhu VI, probably about A.D. 1450, Sapumal Kumāraya invaded Jaffna, but failed to conquer it. He made a second attempt soon after and was successful. After that he ruled this district, but later handed it over to a nephew of the last Tamil king, who accepted the supremacy of the Sinhalese.

During this period the Sinhalese kings seem to have exercised very little power even within their own territories. At least one of them, king Bhuvanekabāhu V, was only a nominal ruler, and the real ruler of the time was the chief, Vīra Alakēśvara. Bhuvanekabāhu II, before he became king, must have wielded much power at Kurunägala, to be able to seize the power from Parākramabāhu III. Vijayabāhu III could not have been quite secure at Dambadeniya, as he lodged the tooth relic at Beligala, to the north-west of Vākirigala. Vijayabāhu IV could not enforce the payment of taxes, and was killed by his general, Mittā. Vijayabāhu VI was carried away by the Chinese.

72. ***Buddhism and Hinduism.*** The unsettled state of the country affected Buddhism too. Four kings of this period had to enforce the rules of discipline on the *bhikkhus*, and expel those who refused to obey. The deterioration of the *Sangha* was no doubt partly due to the disturbances caused by invasions from without and civil strife from within.

In spite of the purification and the reconciliation of opposing sects, the Mahāyānist beliefs did not disappear from Ceylon. The worship of Nātha or Avalōkitēśvara came even into greater prominence, especially from the time of Parākramabāhu VI. This *bōdhisattva* is referred to in many literary works, and some inscriptions show that his image was worshipped in many temples. Another deity that was

THE LAṄKATILAKA VIHĀRA, NEAR GAMPOLA

(*Page 73*)

ŚIVA DEVĀLĒ No. 1, POLONNARUVA

(*See page 73*)

worshipped at this time was Sāman, who is identified by some writers with the *bōdhisattva* Samantabhadra.

The *daḷadā* received even more attention than in the Polonnaruva Period. Kings took great care to keep it in their possession, and a change of capital was followed by the building of a new Daḷadā Māligāva.

The influence of Hinduism also grew during this period. Some of the Siṅhalese kings supported Brāhman priests, and Hindu gods began to be worshipped either in *dēvālas* (temples of the gods) attached to the Buddhist *vihāras*, or in the *vihāras* themselves. In the Laṅkatilaka Vihāra, near Gampola, the images of the Hindu gods were placed between the inner and the outer walls of the building. Siṅhalese writers, too, at this time began to pay their homage not only to the Buddha, the *Dhamma* and to the *Saṅgha*, but also to the Hindu gods, like Brahma, Śiva and others. The *bōdhisattvas*, like Nātha and Sāman, began to be identified with the Hindu gods, Śiva and Lakshman.

73. *Architecture and Sculpture.* The unsettled state of the country and the limited resources of the kings are reflected also in the comparatively small number of the buildings of this period. The Laṅkatilaka and the Gaḍaladeniya Vihāras were the only large buildings put up during this time. The Laṅkatilaka is built of brick and its interior is similar to the buildings of the Polonnaruva Period. The only difference is that there are two ante-chambers to the shrine; and this is enclosed by an outer wall, which makes the building square instead of oblong. The inner temple is the Buddhist *vihāra*, and the surrounding corridor is the temple of the gods. The temple known as Śiva Dēvālē No. 1, at Polonnaruva, was possibly built during the Pāṇḍyan occupation. It is built of stone and belongs to the Pāṇḍyan style of architecture of the thirteenth century. The Gaḍaladeniya Vihāra, along with the Laṅkatilaka, was built by Bhuva-

nekabāhu IV of Gampola. It was the only Buddhist *vihāra* so far built of stone, and it has all the characteristics of the Vijayanagara style of architecture. The style of the stairway at Yāpahuva is Hindu, and probably shows the influence of the later Pāṇḍyan or Vijayanagara style.

74. *Literature.* The only progress to be noted during this period is in the field of literature. The practice of writing in Pāli continued, in spite of the study of Sanskrit, which was the language of the scholars on the Indian continent. The works that appeared were similar to those of the previous period. The *Thūpavaṅsa* is very similar in language, style, and subject-matter to the *Mahābōdhivaṅsa.* The second part of the *Cūlavaṅsa* shows even greater influence of Sanskrit. Two other works on historical subjects are the *Hatthavanagalla Vihāra Vaṅsa*, which deals with the story of Srī Sangabo, and the *Sadhamma Saṅgaha*, a history of Buddhism.

Other Pāli literary works include the *Rasavāhini*, a prose work which contains one hundred and three stories, and the poems, the *Jinatarita*, the *Jinalaṅkāra* and the *Samantakūṭa Vaṇṇanā*, which deals with Adam's Peak. There are also works on grammar and a medical work, called *Bhēsajja Manjūsa*, belonging to this period.

The number of Sinhalese literary works of this period is much greater than in any of the previous periods. Many of them are translations or based upon existing Pāli works. Of such a nature are the Sinhalese prose works, the *Thūpavaṅsaya*, the *Daladā Pūjāvalīya* (based on the *Dāṭhāvaṅsa*), the *Attanagaluvaṅsaya*, the *Mahābōdhivaṅsaya*, the *Saddharmālaṅkāra* (based on *Rasavāhini*), and the *Jātaka.* The *Pūjāvaliya*, like the *Thūpavaṅsaya* gives a good deal of historical matter. The *Nikāya Saṅgraha* is also a similar work, and gives the history of Buddhism and its sects. Another religious work is the *Saddharmaratnākaraya*, a treatise on Buddhism.

There appeared also a number of religious poems. The *Kavsiḷumiṇa*, or *Kusadāvata*, written by King Parākramabāhu, gives the story of the *Kusajātaka*, and is similar in language and style to the *Sasadāvata*. The *Kāvyasēkhara* of Toṭagamuvē Srī Rāhula, and the *Guttila Kāvya*, are also *Jātaka* stories related in verse. Other poems are the *Lōkōpakāraya*, a collection of parables, the *Buduguṇalaṅkāraya*, written in praise of the Buddha and of his teaching, and the *Lōväda Saṅgarāva*, which advises the reader to live in conformity with the teachings of Buddha.

There were also books which dealt with secular subjects. The Siṅhalese grammar, *Sidat Saṅgarāva*, which had a very great influence on later Siṅhalese literature, appeared at the beginning of the fourteenth century. The *Siyabaslakara* is a work on Siṅhalese rhetoric which some place in the tenth century; the *Ruvan Mala*, the *Piyum Mala*, and the *Nāmāvaliya* are works dealing with the meanings of words. The *Yogārṇava* and the *Yōgaratnākara*, both books on medicine, also belong to this period.

A new kind of poem, called *sandēsa*, also appeared at this time. They are more secular than religious, and are written in imitation of Kālidāsa's *Mēghadūta*. They embody a message, as the name implies, to be conveyed by a bird to the shrine of a god, invoking his blessing either on the sovereign or a member of the royal family, or imploring the aid of the god for victory in war. There is always a description of the route taken by the bird, and the poems give much information about towns, villages, and buildings of the time.

The greater use of the Siṅhalese language for purposes of writing during this period was due to various causes. The disappearance of Buddhism from India naturally discouraged the continued use of Pāli. Sanskrit did not take its place, as during this time, owing to the occupation of India by the Muhammadans, its importance decreased.

The use of Sinhalese, on the other hand, was mainly due to the study of Sanskrit. This enriched the Sinhalese language by supplying words and terms it lacked. It led to the study of Āryan dialects, or Prākrits, like Apabhraṅśa. It encouraged the study of grammar, prosody and phonetics, helped scholars to understand Sinhalese better and to make use of it as a vehicle of literature. It also made people study subjects other than religious, like medicine and astrology, in which the laymen, who knew no Pāli or Sanskrit, were interested. And when the literary works of Ceylon ceased to appeal to people in India, the writers naturally adopted Sinhalese, as it was now fit for literature and was best understood by the people.

75. *South India: The Pāṇḍyans.* The people who took most advantage of this unsettled state of the island and the existence of two kingdoms, which were often at war with each other, were the South Indians. As the Chōḷian power declined the Pāṇḍyans gradually regained their independence, and then extended their power over the Chōḷa kingdom. Maravarman Sundara Pāṇḍya (A.D. 1216–1239) fought twice against the Chōḷa king, Rājarāja III (A.D. 1216–1246), in 1220 and 1230, and defeated him on the second occasion. Then the Pallava, Ko-Perum Siṅga, the Chōḷa feudatory, also declared himself independent, fought against Rājarāja III, and made him prisoner. Rājarāja, however, was rescued and restored to power by the Hoysāla Narasiṅha II of Mysore. Narasiṅha continued his war against Pāṇḍya after that, and made an expedition as far as Rāmēśvaram. It is recorded that a king of Ceylon called Parākramabāhu, and three of his officers, lost their lives fighting for Perum Singa against Narasiṅha. He was probably one of the petty kings of Ceylon who ruled at this time.

The Pāṇḍyan king, Jaṭāvarman Sundara Pāṇḍya I, met with greater success against Chōḷa about the middle of the thirteenth century. He defeated the Chōḷa and the Hoysāla kings, and made Chōla subordinate to him. He claimed to have invaded Ceylon (about A.D. 1254), and to have received as tribute gems and elephants from the king of Ceylon. His successor, Jaṭāvarman II, invaded Ceylon about A.D. 1254–1256. He claimed to have killed one king, captured his possessions, and to have received tribute from the other. The first was probably the king of Jaffna, and the second Parākramabāhu II.

The next Pāṇḍyan ruler, Maravarman Kulasēkhara (A.D. 1268–1311) also invaded the Sinhalese kingdom. His first attack was repelled by Bhuvanekabāhu I (A.D. 1273–1284). The second invasion was made by his minister, Āryachakravarti, who captured Yāpahuva and took away the *daladā*, which he delivered to Kulasēkhara; and for about twenty years after this Ceylon seems to have been ruled by the Pāṇḍyans. The next Sinhalese king, Parākramabāhu III, made a personal visit to the Pāṇḍyan king to get back the *daladā*. He probably acknowledged the supremacy of Pāṇḍya and received its protection. The two sons of Kulasēkhara, Vīra and Sundara, fought for the throne at the death of their father. The Muhammadans, under Malik Kāfūr, took this opportunity to conquer the Pāṇḍyan kingdom. Perhaps it was these incidents that led Bhuvanekabāhu II to fight Parākramabāhu III and become king.

76. *The Vijayanagara Empire.* The Muhammadans who conquered Pāṇḍya in A.D. 1310 did not interfere with Ceylon, but their rule came to an end in 1377, when this territory fell into the hands of the Vijayanagara kings, who ruled over India south of the Kṛishṇā and the Tungabhadra. Virupāksha, the son of the Vijayanagara king, Harihāra II (A.D. 1399–1406), claimed to have conquered Ceylon, but what he conquered was probably only the Jaffna kingdom, for it paid tribute to the Vijayanagara empire, at least while it was ruled by Dēva Rāya II (A.D. 1421–1449). Dēva Rāya II is

said to have invaded Ceylon towards the end of his reign. It was his death, and the subsequent disorder in the government of his country, that probably made it possible for Sapumal Kumāraya to conquer Jaffna, and for the Siṅhalese to make an expedition to Adriampet in South India, on the seizure of a Siṅhalese ship laden with cinnamon, and fight with some success. The Vijayanagara empire lasted till 1565, when it was overthrown by the Muhammadans.

77. *The Malays.* Ceylon was invaded twice during this period also by a Malay Buddhist, called Chandrabhānu, the ruler of Tāmbralinga, a state in the Malay Peninsula near the Bay of Bandon. He made his first invasion in 1244, in the reign of Parākramabāhu II, probably with the object of seizing an image of the Buddha which was said to possess miraculous powers. When he was defeated he went to South India, and came once more in the reign of Vijayabāhu IV, this time with Pāṇḍyan and Chōḷian troops; and demanded the *daladā* and the bowl of the Buddha. He advanced as far as Yāpahuva, but was defeated there by the king's nephew, Vīrabāhu.

78. *China.* The *daladā* was demanded on several occasions also by Chinese emperors, but without success. Kublai Khan, who established the Yuan Dynasty (A.D. 1280–1368), sent for it in A.D. 1284, and envoys came for it twice more in the next century. In A.D. 1405 the Chinese eunuch, Ching Ho, came to Ceylon at the request of the emperor, Yung Ho, of the Ming dynasty (A.D. 1368–1644), to take away the *daladā*, and was treated badly by Vijayabāhu VI. He came again in A.D. 1408, captured the king, the queen, and the officers, and took them to China. Vijayabāhu was released later, and from this time till A.D. 1459 Ceylon seems to have paid tribute to China.

79. *Yemen, Egypt and Pegu.* Ceylon had direct relations also with Yemen, Egypt and Pegu. The king of Jaffna, who

was an ally of the Sultan of Coromandel, was also an ally of the king of Yemen, in Arabia, with which country Ceylon had trade dealings. Bhuvanekabāhu I sought an alliance in A.D. 1283 with Egypt, probably because Yemen was friendly with the Jaffna kingdom, and offered to export precious stones, elephants and cinnamon.

The relations with Burma were not commercial but religious. Dhammazedi, ruler of Pegu (A.D. 1472–1492), sent twenty-two *bhikkhus*, in order to secure valid ordination from the *Saṅgha* of Ceylon. On their return they bestowed the ordination on those who came from Burma and Siam.

The commercial relations with Yemen and South India led to the settlement of a large number of Muhammadans in Ceylon. They penetrated even into the interior of the island, and set up mosques in the villages where they lived. They, too, visited Adam's Peak, as they believed the depression on the top of the peak to be a footmark of Adam. Their chief settlement continued to be Colombo, where a Muhammadan pirate with an Abyssinian garrison controlled the trade.

EPILOGUE

THE last chapter gave an account of the beginning of the decline of the Siṅhalese kingdom, and the history of Ceylon henceforth is the story of this decline. The Portuguese take the place of the Pāṇḍyans, force the Siṅhalese back to the highlands, and capture the Jaffna kingdom from the Tamils. The Dutch capture the maritime districts from the Portuguese; and the British, who in turn take them from the Dutch, also capture the mountainous district and put an end to Siṅhalese independence.

The narrative is not continued, like the *Mahāvaṅsa*, up to the conquest of Ceylon by the British. The arrival of the Portuguese in Ceylon is a better place to stop, as it is the turning-point from the medieval into the modern period. From this time the people of Ceylon begin to look more to the West than to India for its progress, and the influence of Hinduism is gradually replaced by that of Christianity. They also begin to adopt western methods and customs, and lay the foundations for the great advance made in the last hundred years.

There is no doubt that Ceylon has changed vastly since the British occupation, and some of the most significant features of its modern life have had their beginnings only in recent times. The new forces at work have transformed the life of the people considerably, and Ceylon is once more at a fresh turning-point in its history.

Nevertheless, in spite of these great changes, many of the old forces are still at work. Though the study of the English language and literature has given the people to some extent a new outlook on life, the languages which are yet most widely used are Sinhalese and Tamil. Though the influence of the Christian Church is quite out of proportion to its numbers, Buddhism and Hinduism have still far more adherents, and the number of the Muhammadans is not much less than that of the Christians. Though agriculture is carried on today more for commercial purposes, rice-cultivation is still the occupation of a large number of people. Though the railway, the motor car, the telegraph, and the telephone have become an inseparable part of the life of the people, and have helped the Government to spread its tentacles in every direction, affecting almost every aspect of life, yet some of the old methods of travelling and some of the old forms of administration have not yet disappeared. Moreover, there is now a revived interest in the old forms of architecture, sculpture, and painting. More attention is being paid to the restoration of old tanks and channels. And there is a tendency on the part of some to look to India once more for their inspiration.

It is not possible for the people of Ceylon to break away altogether from its past history, for the roots of the present lie too deep for that, and some of the factors, such as the geographical conditions, that influenced Ceylon in the past, have not changed very considerably. The people of Ceylon, like all living organisms, cannot ignore their past. They can only change, adapting themselves to new conditions. What is important is that they should preserve what is of enduring value, abandon what is obsolete, and absorb from without whatever is necessary for their growth. Hence the time was never more opportune for a correct appreciation of the past heritage of Ceylon, and this book will serve its purpose if it helps the people of this island, even in a small way, to obtain a better understanding of their past history.

APPENDIX I

LIST OF KINGS, WITH DATES[1]

NO.		B.C.
1.	Vijaya	483
	Interregnum of one year	445
2.	Paṇḍuvasdev (Paṇḍuvāsudēva), nephew of 1 ...	444
3.	Abhaya, son of 2	414
	Interregnum	394
4.	Paṇḍukābhaya, nephew of 3	377
5.	Muṭasiva, son of 4	307
6.	Dēvānaṁpiya Tissa (Devanapā Tis), second son of 5	247
7.	Uttiya, brother of 6	207
8.	Mahāsiva, brother of 6	197
9.	Sūra Tissa, brother of 6	187
10 and 11.	Sēna and Guttika, Tamils	177
12.	Asela, brother of 6	155
13.	Eḷāra (Eḷāla), Tamil	145
14.	Duṭugämunu (Duṭṭhagāmaṇi)	101
15.	Saddhā Tissa (Sādā Tis, Gamiṇi Tisa), brother of 14	77
16.	Tullatthana (Thūlathana, Tulnā), son of 15 ...	59
17.	Lajjitissa (Lañjatissa, Lāmāni Tis, Tisa Abaya), brother of 16	59
18.	Khallāṭanāga (Kaḷunna), brother of 16	50
19.	Vaḷagambā (Vaṭṭagāmaṇi Abhaya, Gamaṇi Abaya), brother of 16	43
20–24.	Five Tamils, Puḷahattha, Bāhiya, Panayamāraka, Piḷayamāraka Dāṭhika (Dāṭhiya) ...	43
19.	Vaḷagambā (restored)	29
25.	Mahasiḷu Mahatis (Mahācūḷi Mahātissa, Mahadāliyā Tissa), son of 18	17
26.	Chōra Nāga, son of 19	3
		A.D.
27.	Tissa (Kuḍā Tissa), son of 25	9
28.	Anulā (with Śiva, Vaṭuka, Dārubhatika Tissa and Niliya), widow of 26	12

[1] The dates are based mainly on *Cūlavaṅsa*, Vol. II, pp. ix–xiv, and the names on *Epigraphia Zeylanica*, Vol. III, pp. 1–40.

NO.		A.D.
29.	Makalantissa (Kuṭakaṇṇa Tissa, Kuḍakaṇa, Kāḷakaṇṇi Tissa), brother of 27	16
30.	Bhātiya I (Bhāṭikābhaya, Bhātika Tissa), son of 29 ...	38
31.	Mahadäliya Mānā (Mahādāṭhika Mahānāga), brother of 30	67
32.	Aḍagämuṇu (Āmaṇḍa Gāmaṇi Abhaya), son of 31 ...	79
33.	Kaṇirajānu Tissa (Kiṇihiridaḷa), brother of 32 ...	89
34.	Cūlābhaya (Kuḍā Abā, Suḷu Abhā), son of 32 ...	92
35.	Sīvalī, sister of 34	93
	Interregnum of three years	93
36.	Iḷa Nāga (Eḷunnā), nephew of 35	96
37.	Sandamuhuṇu (Chandamukha Śiva), son of 36 ...	103
38.	Yasalālakatissa (Yasasiḷu), brother of 37	112
39.	Subha (Saba)	120
40.	Vasabha (Vähäp)	127
41.	Vaṅkanāsika Tissa (Vaknähä Tis, Vannäsinambapa), son of 40	171
42.	Gajabā I (Gajabāhuka Gāmaṇi), son of 41	174
43.	Mahaḷunā (Mahallaka Nāga, Mahaḷu Mānā), father-in-law of 42	196
44.	Bhātiya Tissa II (Bhātika Tissa, Bātiya), son of 43 ...	203
45.	Kaniṭu Tis (Kaniṭṭha Tissa, Cūla Tissa), brother of 44	227
46.	Kuhunnā (Khujja Nāga, Suḷunā), son of 45	246
47.	Kuḍḍa Nāga (Kuñca-Nāga, Kuḍānā), brother of 46 ...	248
48.	Siri Nāga I (Sirinā Kuḍā Sirinā), brother-in-law of 47	249
49.	Vēra Tissa (Vohārika Tissa), son of 48	269
50.	Abhaya Nāga (Abā Sen, Abhā Tissa), brother of 49 ...	291
51.	Siri Nāga II (Sirinā), son of 49	300
52.	Vijayindu (Vijaya Kumāraka), son of 51	302
53.	Saṅgha Tissa I	303
54.	Siri Saṅgabō I (Siri Saṅghabōdhi)	307
55.	Goḷu Abā (Gōṭhābhaya, Mēghavaṇṇābhaya) ...	309
56.	Deṭu Tis I (Jeṭṭha Tissa, Kalakan Deṭa Tis, Makalan Deṭa Tis), son of 55	323
57.	Mahasen (Mahāsēna), brother of 56	334
58.	Kit Siri Mevan (Kitti Siri Mēghavaṇṇa), son of 57	362
59.	Deṭu Tis II (Jeṭṭha Tissa), nephew of 58 ...	
60.	Buddhadāsa (Bujas), son of 59	
61.	Upatissa I, son of 60	
62.	Mahānāma, brother of 61	409

NO.		A.D.
63.	Sotthi Sēna (Sengot), son of 62	431
64.	Chhattagāhaka (Satgāhaka, Lämäni Tis), son-in-law of 62	431
65.	Mit Sen (Mittasēna, Karal Sora)	432
66.	Paṇḍu, Tamil	} 433
67.	Parinda, son of 66	
68.	Khudda Pārinda, brother of 67	
69.	Tiritara, Tamil	
70.	Dāṭhiya, Tamil	
71.	Pīṭhiya, Tamil	
72.	Dhātusena, Dāsenkāliya	460
73.	Kāśyapa I (Kassapa, Sīgiri Käsubu, Kasubu), son of 72	478
74.	Mugalan I (Moggallāna), son of 72	496
75.	Kumāra Dās (Kumāra Dhātusena, Kumāra Dāsen), son of 74	513
76.	Kīrti Sēna (Kitti Sēna, Kit Sen), son of 75	522
77.	Śiva (Mädi Śiv), uncle of 76	522
78.	Upatissa II (Lämäni Upatissa), son-in-law of 72 ...	524
79.	Silākāla (Salamevan), son-in-law of 72	524
80.	Dāpuḷu Sen (Dāṭhāpabhuti), second son of 79 ...	537
81.	Mugalan II (Moggallāna, Cūla Moggallāna, Daḷa Mugalan), elder brother of 80	537
82.	Kit Siri Mē (Kitti Siri Megha, Kuḍā Kit Siri Mevan), son of 81	556
83.	Mahānāga (Senevi Mānā)	556
84.	Agbō I (Aggabōdhi, Akbō), nephew of 83	568
85.	Agbō II (Aggabōdhi, Kudā Akbō), nephew of 84 ...	601
86.	Saṅgha Tissa II	611
87.	Daḷa Mugalan (Dalla Moggallāna, Lämäni Bō Nā Mugalan, Mädi Bō Mugalan)	611
88.	Silāmeghavarṇa (Silāmeghavaṇṇa, Salamevan) ...	617
89.	Agbō III (Aggabōdhi, Siri Saṅgabō), son of 88	} 626
90.	Deṭu Tis II (Jeṭṭha Tissa, Lämäni Kaṭusara Deṭa Tis), son of 86	
	Agbō III (restored)	
91.	Dāṭhōpa Tissa I (Dāṭhāsiva, Lämäni Daḷupa Tis)	
92.	Kāśyapa II (Kassapa, Päsuḷu Kasubu), brother of 89...	641
93.	Dappula I (Dāpulu), son-in-law of 88	650
94.	Dāṭhōpa Tissa II (Hatthadāṭha, Lämäni Daḷupa Tis), nephew of 91	650

NO.		A.D.
95.	Agbō IV (Aggabōdhi, Siri Saṅgabo), brother of 94 ...	658
96.	Datta (Valpiṭi-väsi-Dat)	674
97.	Hatthadāṭha (Huṇannaru-riyan daḷa)	676
98.	Mānavamma (Mahalā-pāṇō), son of 92	676
99.	Agbō V (Aggabōdhi, Akbō), son of 98	711
100.	Kāśyapa III (Kassapa, Kasubu), brother of 99 ...	717
101.	Mihindu I (Mahinda, Midelraja), brother of 99 ...	724
102.	Agbō VI (Aggabōdhi Silāmegha, Akbō-Salamevan), son of 100	727
103.	Agbō VII (Aggabōdhi, Kuḍā Akbō), son of 101 ...	766
104.	Mihindu II (Mahinda Silāmēgha, Salamevan Mihindu), son of 102	772
105.	Dappula II (Udaya, Dāpulu, Udā rāja), son of 104 ...	792
106.	Mihindu III (Mahinda, Dhammika Silāmēgha, Häligäravil Hiskä sō Mihindu), son of 105	797
107.	Agbō VIII (Aggabōdhi, Mädi Akbō), brother of 106	801
108.	Dappula III (Dāpulu), brother of 106	812
109.	Agbō IX (Aggabōdhi, Päsulu Akbō), son of 108 ...	828
110.	Sēna I (Silāmēgha, Matvaḷa Sen, Salamevan), brother of 109...	831
111.	Sēna II (Mugayin Sen, Abhā Siri Saṅgabō), nephew of 110...	851
112.	Udaya (Udā Abhā Salamevan), brother of 109 ...	885
113.	Kāśyapa IV (Kassapa, Kasup, Kasub Siri Sangabō), brother of 111	896
114.	Kāśyapa V (Kassapa Kasup, Päsulu Kasubu, Salameyvan Abahay), son of 111	913
115.	Dappula IV (Dāpulu), brother of 114	923
116.	Dappula V (Kuḍā Dāpulu, Buddas Abahay Salamevan Dāpula), brother of 114	923
117.	Udaya II (Udā), nephew of 111	934
118.	Sēna III (Sen), brother of 117	937
119.	Udaya III (Udā), brother of 117	945
120.	Sēna IV (Päsulu or Mädi Sen), son of 114	953
121.	Mihindu IV (Mahinda, Kuḍā Midel, Midel Salā), brother of 120	956
122.	Sēna V (Salamevan), son of 121	972
123.	Mihindu V (Mahinda), brother of 122	981
	Interregnum of twelve years	1017
124.	Vikramabāhu (Kassapa, Kāśyapa), son of 123 ...	1029

NO.		A.D.
125.	Kīrti (Kitti)	1041
126.	Mahālāṇa Kīrti (Mahālāṇa Kitti, Mahalē)	1041
127.	Vikrama Pāṇḍu (Vikum Paṇḍi)	1044
128.	Jagatpāla (Jagatīpāla)	1047
129.	Parākrama Pāṇḍu I (Pärakum)	1051
130.	Lokēśvara (Loka, Lokissara)	1053
131.	Kāśyapa (Kassapa, Kasub)[1]	1059
132.	Vijayabāhu I (Kitti), grandson of 124	1059
133.	Jayabāhu I, brother of 132	1114
134.	Vikramabāhu I, son of 132	1116
135.	Gajabāhu II, son of 134	1137
136.	Parākramabāhu I	1153
137.	Vijayabāhu II, son of 135	1186
138.	Mihindu VI (Mahinda)	1187
139.	Kīrti Niśśanka Malla	1187
140.	Vīrabāhu I, son of 139	1196
141.	Vikramabāhu III, brother of 139	1196
142.	Choḍagaṅga, nephew of 139	1196
143.	Līlāvatī, queen of 136 (with Kīrti)	1197
144.	Sāhasa Malla, brother of 139	1200
145.	Kalyāṇavatī, queen of 139 (with Āyasmanta Camūpati)	1202
146.	Dharmāśoka	1208
147.	Anikaṅga (Aniyaṅga)	1209
143.	Līlāvatī (with Vikkantacamūnakka)	1209
148.	Lokēśvara (Lokissara)	1210
143.	Līlāvatī	1211
149.	Parākrama Pāṇḍu (Pärakum Paṇḍi)	1211
150.	Magha	1214–1235
151.	Vijayabāhu III (Vijayabāhu-vat himi)	1232
152.	Parākramabāhu II (Kalikāla Sāhitya Sarvajña Paṇḍita Parākrambāhu), son of 151	1236
153.	Vijayabāhu IV (Bosat Vijayabāhu), son of 152 ...	1271
154.	Bhuvanekabāhu I (Lokekabāhu), brother of 153 ...	1273
	Interregnum	1284
155.	Parākramabāhu III, son of 153	1302
156.	Bhuvanekabāhu II (Vat-himi Bhuvanekabāhu), son of 154...	1310

[1] Nos. 124–131 were rulers of Ruhuṇa. The capital of 127 was Kalutara and Kataragama was the capital of 131 and 132.

NO.		A.D.
157.	Parākramabāhu IV (Paṇḍita Parākramabāhu), son of 156	1325
158.	Bhuvanekabāhu III (Vanni Bhuvanekabāhu)	
159.	Vijayabāhu V (Jayabāhu, Savuḷu Vijayabāhu)	
160.	Bhuvanekabāhu IV	1346–1353
161.	Parākramabāhu V (Savuḷu Pärākum) son of 159	1348–1360
162.	Vikramabāhu III	1347–1375
163.	Bhuvanekabāhu V	1360–1391
164.	Vīrabāhu II, brother-in-law of 163... ...	1391–1397
165.	Vijayabāhu VI (Vīra Alakeśvara), brother of 164	1397–1409
166.	Parākramabāhu Apā	1409–1412
167.	Parākramabāhu VI	1412–1468
168.	Jayabāhu II (Vīra Parākramabāhu) ...	1468–1473
169.	Bhuvanekabāhu VI (Sapumal Kumāraya), son of 167...	1473–1480
170.	Parākramabāhu VII (Paṇḍita Parākramabāhu)	1480–1484
171.	Parākramabāhu VIII (Ambulugala rāja) ...	1484–1518

APPENDIX II

KEY TO ILLUSTRATION: THE DEVELOPMENT OF THE SIṄHALESE SCRIPT

1. Beginning of Aśōka's Second Rock-Edict, from Girnār, in Western India:

Text: (1) Sarvata vijitamhi Devānaṁpriyasa Priyadasino rāño; (2) evamapi pracaṅtesu yathā Coḍā Pāḍā Satiyaputo Ketalaputo ā Tamba; (3) paṅṇī.

Translation: Everywhere in the dominions of King Dēvānampriya Priyadarśin, and likewise among (his) borderers, such as the Cōḍas, the Pāṇḍyas, the Satiyaputa, the Ketalaputa, even Tāmraparṇī.

2. An inscription in a cave at Mihintalē, reading from right to left; two letters turned upside down:

Text: Upaśika Tiśaya leṇe.

Translation: The cave of the lay-devotee, Tissa.

3. An inscription in a cave at Riṭigala, in the North-Central Province:

Text: Devanapiya maharajha Gamiṇi Tisaha puta Devanapiya Tisa A (bayaha) leṇe agata anagata catu (di) disa śagaśa.

Translation: The cave of Devanapiya Tisa Abaya, son of the great king, Devanapiya Gamiṇi Tisa (is given) to the Buddhist priesthood from the four quarters, present and not present. (D. Tisa Abaya = Lañjitissa and D. Gamiṇi Tisa = Saddhā Tissa.)

4. Beginning of an inscription of Bhātika Abhaya, from Mōlāhiṭiya velēgale, in the Tamankaḍuva District:

Text: (Svastika symbol) Siddham Devanapiya Tisa maharajaha marumanaka Kuḍakaṇa-rajaha jeta-pute raja-Abaye.

Translation: King Abhaya, grandson of the great King Devanapiya Tisa, eldest son of King Kuḍakaṇa.

5. Lines 9 and 10 of the Vessagiriya slab-inscription of Dappula V:

Text: Mapurum—Buddas—Abahay—Salamevan Dāpula-maharajhu sat—läṅgūdevana—havuruduyehi.

Translation: In the second year after the umbrella was raised by His Majesty the great King Buddas Abahay Salamevan Dāpuḷa.

6. An inscription on a pillar standing on the embankment of the Padaviya tank in the North-Central Province:

Text: (1) Bäñda nī ganga väva si—
(2) ri Lakäda ket ka—
(3) ravā siyal diya
(4) randavā Pärākumbā
(5) nirindu keḷe mē.

This inscription is in verse.

Translation: Having dammed up smaller streams, rivers (and constructed) tanks in Srī Lankā (and) caused fields to be cultivated (and) all the water to be retained (in the tanks), King Parākramabāhu made this.

Zeitschrift für Indologie und Iranistik.
Zeitschrift der Deutschen Morgenlandes Gesellschaft.
Wiener Zeitschrift für die Kunde des Morgenlandes.
Asia Major.
Journal Asiatique.
Bijdragen de tot taal-landen volken-kunde van Nederlandsch Indie.

INDEX